TWO INCOMES AND STILL BROKE?

TWO INCOMES AND STILL BROKE?

It's Not How Much You Make, but How Much You Keep

LINDA KELLEY

TIMES BOOKS
RANDOM HOUSE

For all exhausted
two-income couples who haven't had time to
smell (or grow) the roses—or
the money to buy them

The case examples in this book are composites of the author, her friends, and acquaintances. Any resemblance to a specific individual is purely coincidental.

The tax examples contained in this publication are not intended to substitute for professional advice. The author is in no way engaged in rendering tax or accounting services. Competent professional assistance is recommended if readers have *any* problems understanding the tax information provided in this book.

Published in the United States by Times Books, a division of Random House, Inc., New York, and simultaneously in Canada by Random House of Canada Limited, Toronto.

This work was originally published in hardcover by Times Books, a division of Random House, Inc., in 1996.

Grateful acknowledgment is made to Ann Landers and Creators Syndicate for permission to reprint one Ann Landers column from December 24, 1989. Copyright © 1989 by Creators Syndicate. Reprinted by permission of Ann Landers and Creators Syndicate.

ISBN 0-8129-2989-6

Random House website address: www.randomhouse.com

Printed in the United States of America on acid-free paper

9 8 7 6 5 4 3 2

First Paperback Edition

Acknowledgments

More than any other person, I would like to thank my husband, Jim, for his support and encouragement. He believed in this book from the day I first suggested writing it—and even before, during all those years when he understood the math of what job expenses could do to us. It takes two to keep the books balanced in a marriage, and Jim's helped me balance them.

I'd also like to thank my agent, Rhoda Weyr, for her advice and encouragement, and Betsy Rapoport, my editor at Times Books, whose enthusiasm and prodding kept me writing when I thought I'd said it all. I give Betsy credit for much of this book that I might not have included except for her nudging to comment, explain, and add more examples. Her personal interest and commitment shine through in many ways, especially in a thinly disguised mention of her own lunch and coffee-break expenses.

Many thanks as well to Susan Krehbiel William, CPA, J.D., Topeka, Kansas, for her helpful answers to my many questions regarding tax matters. Her patience with my many phone calls deserves special mention.

And finally, I'd like to thank all my friends, relatives, and acquaintances who have contributed by sharing their experiences and problems. Their good sense, sound advice, and special insights have contributed greatly to helping me define the difficulties of the two-income life.

Contents

Preface

"Two can live as cheaply as one" was a popular saying when Grandma and Grandpa began married life. Not so gently the real world educated their generation, and slowly one untruth began to blend into another. Now, most of today's young couples are convinced of another misconception: "Two incomes are better than one!" Couples of the nineties take for granted that to attain happiness, self-esteem, and especially a decent standard of living, both partners must work full-time.

Unfortunately, money problems can't always be solved by adding a second income to a family's budget. It's risky to automatically assume another income will balance the books or provide the wherewithal for a better life. For most families there are monetary benefits, although not usually as many as expected, if both partners work outside the home. For others, the effort is wasted in a flow of job expenses that devour the second income and leave nothing but a bewildered and angry couple arguing over where the extra money went.

Of course, money isn't the only justifiable reason to work outside the home. Many choose the work world for the challenge, the excitement, the satisfaction, the desire to make a difference. Others choose to work out of boredom or frustration with what's at home—whether that be an empty, lonely house, or one filled with clamoring children and a live-in mother-in-law. More often than recognized, our work objectives encompass a mixture of motives that include money, satisfaction, and escape from domestic doldrums. Yet no matter what the incentive for your joining the workforce, you should know your paycheck's real worth.

For those of you working so hard for the dollars yet wondering where the money goes, this book will show how an income—especially a family's second income—can mysteriously end up with little or no financial value after job-related expenses (JREs) are subtracted. First incomes have expenses; second incomes have EXPENSES! Most often the economic losers are families with child-care expenses, but a host of other costs in today's complex economy also can wipe out a second income. A questionable second income gives new meaning to the term *money laundering.* Like a washing machine switched from small load to large, more water (income) pours in, whirls and agitates, then drains away.

This book will help you "second incomers" identify the often invisible costs that make it so difficult to determine the true dollar value of your earnings. You may even find that those extra paychecks are actually *costing* you money. Alternatively, you may discover that reduced work hours or even a lower-paying and less-stressful job will, in the end, give you a higher standard of living. No matter what your financial situation or goals, I hope you'll find this book invaluable in evaluating the true worth of your paychecks so that you do not spend beyond your family's means.

As family and community responsibilities increase many two-income families find themselves struggling like the "bone-weary" woman who wrote to Ann Landers in the late 1980s:

'80s woman getting tired

DEAR ANN: I am tired—not just "tired," but bone-weary exhausted. I'm the female of the '80s, a professional woman with a good husband and three wonderful children. I put in 40 hours a week downtown and just as many at home. When people like me are written up in a women's magazine or a newspaper article, you'd think we had the world by the tail. Baloney.

My job as a supervisor is stressful. The demands on me are awesome. Everyone wants something. When I come home I must prepare supper, clean the house, wash clothes, pick up the kids from the activity of the day, help them with homework, see that they are bathed and put to bed. By then, I am totally shot. My body says rest, but my mind says I must get ready for tomorrow.

I am 45 pounds overweight, and every week I add another pound or two. This is another area of my life that I can't seem to control. I know I should go on a diet, but I don't feel like tackling another big job right now.

My husband helps more than most husbands, and the children are our top priority. I truly wish I didn't have to work, but there's no way we could make it if I stayed home. I'm not working so we can have a Mercedes, a pool or fancy vacations. I work so we can meet our house and car payments, buy decent clothes and put food on the table. We are not extravagant people. Even though my husband and I are both professionals, we don't make a great deal of money. If I quit work, it would cut our income in half.

I miss not picking up my kids after school. I was depressed all summer because I couldn't stay at home with them. Before I know it, these children won't need me and I'll have missed it all.

My parents live across town. They are retired and depend on me a lot. This is another heavy burden. They were terrific parents. I feel guilty that I can't do more for them.

My point is this: I'm being pulled every which way by people I feel responsible for. I know you will suggest counseling, Ann, but I live in a rural area and the closest counselor is 55 miles away. With my work and family and limited income, counseling isn't possible.

My pastor tells me I should "pray about it." My doctor says other than occasional hypertension due to my weight and stress, I'm as healthy as a horse.

So, there you have it. Each day is busier than the day before. I feel as if I am sinking in quicksand. I know I have a lot of company. More and more women are juggling jobs and families. Are there any answers for us? I'd like to know what Ann Landers has to say. How in the world did YOU do it?—Tired in Texas.

DEAR TIRED: Please don't look at me as an example of a woman who "did it." There were no sacrifices and no heroics involved.

I was 37 years old when I started to write this column. I had never held a job before, and my daughter was in high school. I had plenty of household help, a supportive husband, and there were no money problems.

I am awe-struck when I read how hard millions of women work at their jobs and then come home to another full-time job. I don't know how they manage. I'm not at all sure I could do it. Let me hear from you. How do YOU do it? I'll print the best letters.

The responses didn't offer much hope. Advice ranged from getting better organized to getting more help from husband and children, and from lowering standard of living to lowering standard of cleanliness. Ubiquitous, one-paragraph revelations that proclaim to solve dual-income couples' time, money, and ideology problems invariably offer naive, oversimplified answers. "Tired in Texas" and millions of her coworkers are still out there, "sinking in quicksand"!

Spurred by the challenge and hopes of a better living standard, wives and mothers have flooded the workforce. In 1960 only 19 percent of married women with children under age six worked outside the home; today that number hovers around 60 percent. Doubtful recruits are persuaded via television characters like Clair Huxtable

(*The Cosby Show*), Elyse Keaton (*Family Ties*), and Maggie Seaver (*Growing Pains*). They make it look *so* easy! Their homes and looks have a surreal orderliness, which magically never needs attending; and they always have time to happily endure the witty escapades of their offspring while they synchronize exciting careers as a lawyer, an architect, and a journalist. Their perfect lives epitomize the American ideal with which everyone wants to identify. Missing from the Huxtables', Keatons', and Seavers' programs are the tight schedules, stress, exhaustion, and frustration that dual careers impose; and their shows leave a legacy of guilt for those who don't measure up to their TV lives.

TV's Roseanne may be on the leading edge of unmasking the perils of having (doing) it all. But she's slovenly and abrasive and her TV-life time, money, and family problems seem *funny*. Perhaps we would identify and see a message too near reality if a disheveled Maggie Seaver played Roseanne's role.

Still, frustration from the race against the clock in two-income families is sometimes ranked second to the

cathy® **by Cathy Guisewite**

IF I DON'T WORK, WE CAN'T PAY ALL OUR BILLS... IF I DO WORK, IT TAKES MOST OF WHAT I MAKE TO PAY FOR DAY CARE.
IF I DON'T WORK, I GET CLAUSTROPHOBIC AND CRANKY. IF I DO WORK, I FEEL LIKE I'M DESERTING HER.
MOMMY'S ON THE GUILT-TRACK.

disappointment of not making it financially after working so hard for two paychecks. (And the reasoning follows, "If we're not making it now on two incomes, how much worse would it be with only one income?!") Most Americans believe their families need incomes of *at least* $20,000 per year just to survive, $30,000 to live moderately, and $50,000 to live comfortably. How high your income must be, of course, depends on where you live, the size of your family, and your personal standards. But, as explained later, a $30,000 first income plus a $20,000 second income will almost *never* add up to a $50,000 lifestyle.

A melee on an *Oprah Winfrey* show illustrates the volatility of the two-income debate. An audience member shouted the popular war cry, "Working mothers just work to buy BMWs!" The passionate, angry responses from working women shook the studio—"We work to make ends meet, to put food on the table, to pay the bills, . . ."—testifying that most second incomes are used for essentials rather than luxuries. The audience's responses make it seem that most budgets built around two incomes have little hope of scaling back to one income.

That's what I call the "two-income myth." This book provides a closer look at those second incomes. They are not always as profitable or as indispensable as they first appear. When one income can't pay the bills, the first antidote normally applied is a second paycheck—sometimes with disappointing results. Couples on the two-income treadmill should consider the old adage, "It's not how much you make, but how much you *keep.*" It is possible to throw out more with spoons than the two of you can haul home in shovels. On a larger scale, our government illustrates how spoons and shovels can work against each other. Our elected officials always manage to "spoon" more out of the Washington money bin than taxpayers can "shovel" into it. Increasing your income doesn't necessarily solve your money problems.

Second incomes are often overrated in terms of net value or spendable income. Spendable income is what remains of a paycheck to spend on financial goals after all job-related expenses are subtracted. It's not generally recognized that second incomes are subject to larger and more JREs than first incomes. This may be because identifying JREs is such a complex undertaking. You've doubtless budgeted for the easy-to-see expenses such as child care and an extra wardrobe. Most other expenses are intangible and often stem from a lack of time to spend and manage assets with thought and deliberation. But Uncle Sam's pickpocket tactics on second incomes are the real scandal. He meticulously camouflages the fact that second incomes almost always pay higher effective tax rates than first incomes, and his well-hidden take is often the decisive factor in measuring a second paycheck's worth. This book will explain in depth the many, often invisible, costs that can reduce second paychecks to *nothing* or less and turn family budgets into a tangle of confusion.

To be expected, JREs vary among jobs and among workers. It's possible for two workers earning the same salary at the same job to have large differences in spendable income. It's also possible for a low-income worker to have a higher *spendable* income than a high-income worker. When you take the time to identify JREs accurately, you'll probably uncover a disappointing lack of spending power, which explains why so many two-income couples aren't doing any better financially than their one-income neighbors. (Of course, single workers can also benefit from learning how to evaluate their paychecks. But single parents with one income pay different tax rates and have more tax breaks than second incomers. Thus, the after-tax value of their incomes is usually higher, and by necessity, their decisions are limited by the lack of another source of income.)

Almost everyone's work motives list includes an increase in income. Rightly or not, our jobs (and incomes) have come to define who we are both to society and to ourselves. Establishing the value of your paycheck may help you decide if satisfaction from working is worth the stress of juggling both home and job responsibilities, or if you need to find a different job with a better bottom line. Decisions will depend a lot on the emphasis you place on income and your overall satisfaction level with your present job and self.

I'm expecting that there will be protests against my associating men (a.k.a. husbands) as first incomers and women (a.k.a. wives and mothers) as second incomers. So, let me explain these definitions. I define *second income,* in most cases, as the supplementary, or lesser income. While we're much closer to the Age of Enlightenment, it's unfortunately still true that women make only about 73 cents for every dollar men earn. Thus, in dual-income marriages, wives' incomes are more often lower than husbands' incomes. Clearly, however, this isn't true across the board; in more and more marriages, the wife's income exceeds that of her husband, and his income could therefore be counted the second income. Still, the majority of second incomes today are earned by women. Most of the examples I use in this book reflect that economic reality.

Nonetheless, I didn't write this book to speak only to women bringing home the second pound of bacon. Even the larger/lesser definition of first/second incomes can be turned about. If the partner earning the larger income wishes to cut back on work hours to write a novel, stay home with the kids, volunteer more in the community, reconnect with his or her inner self, run for political office . . . , his or her income can be counted as second or supplementary so that the economic result of dropping that income can be identified. The larger income can also be listed as second if it's lost due to involuntary layoff or restructuring or downsizing of the workplace—whatever they call it these days. The income loss may not be as serious as anticipated, especially if the laid-off partner is willing to *work* at home managing the family's remaining income. The point is that you should know what each of your two incomes is really worth from both angles so you can make the best choices. Too many dreams are lost because of the unquestioned assumption that "We've both got to work to float our boat."

Yet, in all honesty, I expect this book to be of special interest to working mothers. This is because studies consistently show that it is these women who most often work what sociologist Arlie Hochschild calls "the second shift"—long hours at the office followed by long hours running the household and tending to the kids—thirty-five after-work hours per week, according to recent research. Ideally, at-home duties should be split fifty-fifty between both partners, but the evidence today is that most of that burden falls on Mom. If you're a double-duty, double-stressed Mom, it's important for you to find out what your job is really contributing to the quality of your life and to that of your family.

The last thing I want is for readers to take the message of this book to be "Working mothers belong at home with the kids because their paychecks aren't worth the bother." First off, I think that's a sexist outlook; if you and your partner work through this book together and, for whatever reason, decide that two incomes aren't worth it, who's to say that the ideal answer wouldn't be for Dad to stay home with the kids? Only you know what will work best for you and your family.

More important, you can't decide the true worth of a job based on dollars and cents alone. This book can help you put a dollar value on your job, but it's up to you to put a value on the intangibles that add up to a good life. Every individual must find the right balance between work and home, and define his or her own values and goals.

It should be stressed, part-time work or full-time homemaking are *not* exemptions from sharing financial responsibilities. Efficiently managing a budget on less than two full-time paychecks *is* work, but it takes *time,* the missing ingredient in most two-income marriages. Nevertheless, economic disaster is assured for readers who quit nine to five jobs in favor of reusing aluminum foil and turning off electric lights. Modern money management isn't that simple! You must have the tenacity and ability to understand tax planning and preparation, interest rates, insurance policies, warranties, retirement plans, and investment strategies. You don't need a degree in economics or accounting, but you will need to master fundamental principles; two-career families don't often have the time to study these modern problems.

After reading this far, you're probably thinking that my husband, Jim, is a highly paid CEO whose income makes the one-income life a simple exercise. Not so! Jim's a high school teacher, not a high-paying profession, and we've lived this book from all directions.

I worked full-time as a home economist for a utility company the first three years of our marriage while Jim finished his degree. When I was giving cooking demonstrations, an audience member would invariably comment on how lucky my husband was to have married such a great cook. They didn't know that on the *good* nights I cooked hamburgers. Then our first son arrived, and the good nights grew further apart. I was a "supermom impersonator" telling the world that with enough electric gadgets women could do it all—at home and in the job world.

Jim graduated, I quit work, and two more rowdy boys joined our family. The sound of a humming refrigerator became a quirky delight to me that I heard only when Jim took the kids on an outing and left me home alone to enjoy some peace. Somehow we got by on Jim's beginning teacher's salary, but all our pleasures *had* to be those money couldn't buy. Yet I wouldn't trade those years for anything.

After the boys were all in school, I knew it was time to break off my affair with refrigerator noises. But I didn't want to be a supermom impersonator again either. Because I've always strongly believed in "It's not what you make, but what you keep," I carefully charted out the spendable portion of any paycheck I might earn. I was fortunate to find a fun and fulfilling part-time job—three hours a day—working with senior citizens. The low hourly wage turned out to be competitive with full-time paychecks when fringe benefits and low JREs were factored in. Some wonderful friendships came about through that job, and I learned a lot about "the last of life, for which the first was made." A balance was struck. Our family had some extra money, although there's never enough, no matter what you earn. But most important, we had the time to "smell some roses."

It's taken since the mid-sixties, when I was touting how to do it all with help from Redi-Kilowatt, for superwomen to admit the difficulties of balancing full-time work and home. We've been reluctant to admit to what we see and feel—that doing it all is exhausting, and that dollars often determine our career choices.

The question is, if your paycheck is evaporating into JREs, is the hectic life worth it? If not, you might be better off, from both a time and money standpoint, using your abilities to master modern money management skills. And with your free time, maybe you can . . . write a book. Good luck!

TWO INCOMES AND STILL BROKE?

Introduction

When young marrieds Brad and Sally were barely making it on Brad's $30,000 advertising job, the only escape from their economic plateau seemed to be for Sally to return to work. Sally had worked for only a few years before their two children—now ages three and one—were born, but her social worker's salary would add an additional $20,000 per year to their income. They were sure that a $50,000 ($30,000 + $20,000) income bracket would bring better days.

They did some quick figuring to see how much of Sally's income would be left after taxes and child care and estimated they would have an extra $800 a month to spend ($20,000 ÷ 12 months = $1,667 per month – $467 [taxes at 28%] – $400 [child care] = $800). An extra $800 per month made them ecstatic. They bought a nicer home with a mortgage payment of $300 per month more than their old payment. And with the remaining $500, they planned to start a savings plan for their children's education plus have a comfortable amount of extra spending money each month. The first few weeks after Sally returned to work were the happiest days of their lives.

Two years later they were bankrupt and filing for divorce.

WHAT HAPPENED?

Only a few paychecks after Sally returned to work, they realized something was dreadfully wrong with their budget. Instead of just making it, as before, or having $500 extra for a college fund and spending money, as planned, they began running $500 *short* each month. This mysterious money problem provoked an estrangement between Brad and Sally that added to the pressure and strain of juggling tight schedules and caring for two active toddlers. By the time the children were fed, bathed, and vital household duties finished, Brad and Sally dropped into bed each night, exhausted. Their problems began with money. But now they were in the center of a major economic crisis and fighting a time war as well.

Brad thought they were sharing household responsibilities. True, they were both busy every night. Brad helped with the dishes. He also watched and played with the children while Sally worked on the more mundane chores of cooking, laundry, cleaning, and shopping. In her book, *The Second Shift,* sociologist Arlie Hochschild shows that only 18 to 20 percent of husbands share housework equally with their wives. Most, like Brad, contribute in varying degrees and believe—or want their wives to believe—they share fifty-fifty. This division of labor led to a festering resentment that Sally could never express and Brad never recognized.

Sally hoped the time problem would disappear as the children grew older. But friends warned that she and Brad would trade changing diapers and reading bedtime stories for car pooling, helping with homework, car pooling, PTA meetings, car pooling, Little League baseball, car pooling, Girl Scout cookie sales, car pooling, . . . and then, finally, sleepless nights waiting for teenagers to come home. The time issue wasn't going to resolve itself soon.

There was also the money problem—that mysterious $500 deficit. Brad reasoned that child-care expenses would decrease and their money problems would ease when the kids reached school age. His friends cautioned that babysitting bills would be offset by music lessons,

school supplies, mounting grocery bills, braces, summer camp, designer jeans, and, oh yes, college funds. The money problem wasn't going to go away either.

Brad and Sally earnestly searched for an explanation to the money shortage, and they recalled (and embellished) the good times they shared just breaking even before Sally returned to work. Nonetheless, if Sally quit her job, they knew they would still be $300 per month in arrears because of the larger mortgage. The only answer seemed to be to sell their new house and start over. At any cost, they couldn't accept this bitter solution.

So what happened to Sally's $800? Remember, they were supposed to have $300 for a larger mortgage payment and $500 for a college fund and extra spending money ($800 – $300 = $500). Instead they had a $500 *deficit* each month, still had no extra spending money, and were still unable to save for college. One thousand dollars of Brad and Sally's combined income had disappeared because a unique math system had emerged. *When dealing with second incomes, numbers with dollar signs do not add and subtract by regular rules.* Brad's $30,000 income and Sally's $20,000 income did not add up to $50,000.

You may suspect by now that Brad was spending money on another woman or Sally was going to the horse races. In fact, they may have thought that of each other. A second income's disappearance can be as difficult to pin down as a congressman defending pork-barrel legislation. The answers to Brad and Sally's problems lie in the New Math brought about by Sally's job expenses.

HOW TO USE THIS BOOK

This book is divided into thirteen chapters. The first twelve explain in depth how Brad and Sally's money vanished into job-related expenses and will help you identify your own JREs. The Second-Income Job-Related Expenses chart on pages 10 and 11 shows examples of how JREs can influence second incomes ranging between $10,400 and $52,000 per year. Best and Typical cases are shown for each income level. Best examples have near to the lowest JRE profiles possible; Typical examples have a more realistic JRE makeup. Don't be surprised if your own JREs are even greater than the Typical examples, as higher JREs than those shown are very possible. Notice in the chart that the Typical cases all show a negative or questionable bottom line.

The chart examples demonstrate the fatal tendency among most second incomers to spend more on JREs as income rises. Higher income does not just result in higher taxes but also often requires a more stylish work wardrobe and a tendency to spend more on child care, transportation and lunches, timesavers, rushed shopping, and rewards. Conversely, a higher income may provide more employee benefits or perks than a lower income. I'll explain all these in the chapters to follow.

No two jobs are likely to afford the same salary and benefits or have the same JREs. Moreover, every family's circumstances will change the numbers even further; results are about as individual as fingerprints. I've provided a worksheet, Your Second-Income Job-Related Expenses, on pages 12 and 13, to be filled in as you read each chapter. However, since your life changes constantly, your expenses do too; for this reason, it is a good idea to review and update numbers at least annually. You also may use the worksheet for listing JREs on proposed career changes so that you can more accurately measure each job's true economic benefit and make financially intelligent career moves. The numbers are dollars—*your dollars!* Be honest with yourself as you read each chapter and don't rely on a quick estimate as Brad and Sally did.

Determining the true value of a second income is not always easy, primarily because Uncle Sam gets involved in so many ways. He uses smoke and mirror tricks to disguise his real take on second incomes and leaves many couples, like Brad and Sally, making rough estimates on the financial value of their second paycheck. Because of these sophisticated camouflage techniques, it's necessary to become a lot better informed on tax issues than most of us would like to be. Let me emphasize that I'm not a tax expert. My hope is to acquaint you with the relevant tax issues so that you can identify the after-tax value of your income. You may want to get professional help in applying the information to your individual situation.

Chapters 7 through 11 of this book (and a small section in chapter 12, Earned Income Credit) all deal with JREs that are, or may be, influenced by tax laws. You'll need to spend a few quiet hours on these chapters. My explanations provide a streamlined method of estimating the cost of tax-related JREs; they are not intended to be a complete (and boring) guide to tax preparation. You can read the other chapters while you're vacuuming or taking a bath. They'll be easier to read through dust and soapsuds.

JREs are subtracted from gross income to determine spendable income. Spendable income is what remains of gross income to spend on financial goals. In ideal instances, your spendable income will be substantial enough to support your financial goals; in unfortunate cases, such as Sally's, negative spendable income can deter you from achieving economic objectives.

Throughout this book, you will notice confusing gray areas where JREs and financial goals seem to overlap. An appropriate work wardrobe is a JRE, but the wardrobe (or part of it) also might be a financial goal if it befits after-five wear or if you crave an impeccably tailored Armani suit instead of a Brooks Brothers off the rack. When JREs and financial goals intermix, you'll need to apportion costs, according to actual use and conscience, between the two categories.

BRAD AND SALLY'S MONTHLY FINANCIAL GOALS

1. Afford a larger house payment ($300)
2. Begin a savings plan for their children's education ($200)
3. Have a comfortable amount of spending money ($300)

So that you don't confuse your JREs and financial goals in later chapters, list the financial goals you hope to achieve through a second income and their approximate monthly costs on page 14. Add more lines if your list is long.

SECOND-INCOME JOB-RELATED EXPENSES ($)

	$5/Hr. or $10,400/Yr. Best Case	$5/Hr. or $10,400/Yr. Typical Case	$10/Hr. or $20,800/Yr. Best Case	$10/Hr. or $20,800/Yr. Typical Case	$15/Hr. or $31,200/Yr. Best Case
Monthly salary	867	867	1,733	1,733	2,600
Chap. 1 Child care*	0	–300	0	–400	0
Chap. 2 Personal upkeep*	0	–50	0	–100	0
Chap. 3 Trans. and lunches*	0	–50	0	–100	0
Chap. 4 Timesavers*	0	–120	0	–160	0
Chap. 5 Rushed shopping*	–100	–100	–100	–150	–100
Chap. 6 Rewards*	0	–100	0	–150	0
Chap. 7 Federal taxes**	–130	–183	–260	–405	–390
Chap. 8 State taxes†	0	–61	0	–121	0
Chap. 9 Social Security‡	–66	–66	–133	–133	–199
Chap. 10 Deductible job expenses*	0	–30	0	–40	0
Chap. 11 Perks§	150	0	175	0	200
Chap. 12 And what else?*	0	–20	0	–30	0
Chap. 13 The bottom line (monthly spendable income)	721	–213	1,415	–56	2,111

* Most job-related expenses tend to rise with income; the more earned, the more spent. Of course, expenses are also influenced by individual factors, for instance, child-care expense is influenced by the number and ages of children.

** Federal income tax is figured at 15 percent for Best examples and 28 percent for Typical examples. Typical cases—all with child-care expense—have federal taxes reduced $60 to $80 per month to reflect the child-care tax credit. First income often pushes second income into a higher bracket than paid by first income. It's therefore unlikely that higher income Best examples will pay 15 percent. High-income couples may pay rates as steep as 39.6 percent.

SECOND-INCOME JOB-RELATED EXPENSES ($)

	$15/Hr. or $31,200/Yr. Typical Case	$20/Hr. or $41,600/Yr. Best Case	$20/Hr. or $41,600/Yr. Typical Case	$25/Hr. or $52,000/Yr. Best Case	$25/Hr. or $52,000/Yr. Typical Case
Monthly salary	2,600	3,467	3,467	4,333	4,333
Chap. 1 Child care*	–500	0	–600	0	–700
Chap. 2 Personal upkeep*	–150	0	–200	0	–250
Chap. 3 Trans. and lunches*	–150	0	–200	0	–250
Chap. 4 Timesavers*	–200	0	–240	0	–280
Chap. 5 Rushed shopping*	–200	–100	–250	–100	–300
Chap. 6 Rewards*	–200	0	–250	0	–300
Chap. 7 Federal taxes**	–648	–520	–891	–650	–1,133
Chap. 8 State taxes†	–182	0	–243	0	–303
Chap. 9 Social Security‡	–199	–265	–265	–331	–331
Chap. 10 Deductible job expenses*	–50	0	–60	0	–70
Chap. 11 Perks§	0	225	0	250	0
Chap. 12 And what else?*	–40	0	–50	0	–60
Chap. 13 The bottom line (monthly spendable income)	81	2,807	218	3,502	356

† State income tax is figured at the 0 percent rate for Best examples and 7 percent for Typical examples. A few states have no state income tax. Others have rates as high as 12 percent.

‡ Social Security is figured at 7.65 percent for all examples. Self-employed pay a higher rate; see chapter 9.

§ Employee perks or benefits will *usually add* to spendable income. But, they also can subtract; see chapter 11. Generally, employee benefits increase with salary.

YOUR SECOND-INCOME JOB-RELATED EXPENSES ($)

	Job Choice No. 1 $______ per hour $________ per year	Job Choice No. 2 $______ per hour $________ per year	Job Choice No. 3 $______ per hour $________ per year
Monthly salary			
Chap. 1 Child care			
Chap. 2 Personal upkeep			
Chap. 3 Trans. and lunches			
Chap. 4 Timesavers			
Chap. 5 Rushed shopping			
Chap. 6 Rewards			
Chap. 7 Federal taxes			
Chap. 8 State taxes			
Chap. 9 Social Security			
Chap. 10 Deductible job expenses			
Chap. 11 Perks			
Chap. 12 And what else?			
Chap. 13 The bottom line			

YOUR SECOND-INCOME JOB-RELATED EXPENSES ($)

	Job Choice No. 4 $______ per hour $________ per year	Job Choice No. 5 $______ per hour $________ per year	Job Choice No. 6 $______ per hour $________ per year
Monthly salary			
Chap. 1 Child care			
Chap. 2 Personal upkeep			
Chap. 3 Trans. and lunches			
Chap. 4 Timesavers			
Chap. 5 Rushed shopping			
Chap. 6 Rewards			
Chap. 7 Federal taxes			
Chap. 8 State taxes			
Chap. 9 Social Security			
Chap. 10 Deductible job expenses			
Chap. 11 Perks			
Chap. 12 And what else?			
Chap. 13 The bottom line			

YOUR MONTHLY FINANCIAL GOALS

1.____________________________ ($______)
2.____________________________ ($______)
3.____________________________ ($______)

After identifying your true spendable income (see chapter 13, The Bottom Line), you'll know if your second income helps or hinders achievement of the above goals.

A POOR LAWYER!

The Second-Income JREs chart (pages 10–11) shows a waitress (first column, Best Case) earning $5 per hour with spendable income of $721 per month. Ironically, her best-tipping customer, a junior lawyer (last column, Typical Case) who earns $25 per hour, has a spendable income of only $356 per month. How $5 per hour can be worth more than $25 per hour is a mystery that will unfold in later chapters. Realize though, if you're in business for the green stuff, the game's name is not Net Income, Gross Income, Income after Taxes, but SPENDABLE INCOME!

For now, a brief explanation of each person's finances will do. The waitress was fortunate to have a low JRE profile. Her husband's income was small, so it didn't push her income into a higher tax bracket; she lived within walking distance of the restaurant; the restaurant provided employees free coffee and lunches; Grandma lived next door and took care of the children; her uniforms were furnished; she did her own hair; and the restaurant paid most of her health insurance.

The lawyer was not so fortunate. Because she believed her position required her to be involved in community activities, she often worked sixty-hour weeks between practicing law and public service projects. As a consequence, she had the extra expense for household help, and of course, she paid more in taxes than the waitress. She also had to dress to project the right image, drive a car that projected the right image, send her son to a day care that . . . As a reward for the hectic pace they kept, she and her husband took mini-vacations several times a year to get away from responsibilities and the ringing telephone. Her health-insurance benefit was of no value because her family was already covered by an excellent plan through her husband's employment. Lastly, she spent a small sum on counseling to help her handle the stress and difficulties she had with time management.

Most readers will fall somewhere between the waitress's and the lawyer's circumstances. But for everyone, much soul-searching is necessary to accurately classify expenses. The lawyer's vacation expense might have been a financial goal, but she confessed it was more truly an escape from her hectic life and thus a JRE. The BMW she drove was more closely linked to her image as a successful lawyer than a financial goal, and thus a large portion of its cost was a JRE.

BACK TO BRAD AND SALLY

Okay, where did Sally's money go? You've probably got a vague idea by now. Later chapters will explain Sally's monthly expenses in detail, but expenses Brad and Sally forgot about or misjudged were briefly as follows:

SALLY'S MONTHLY JOB-RELATED EXPENSES

Child care	\$542	They spent \$130 per week × 50 weeks = \$6,500 ÷ 12 months = \$542 per month. They received a tax credit for child-care expense of \$960, which was subtracted from their federal income tax.
Personal upkeep	\$125	Sally was a sweatshirt-and-jeans person before she returned to work. Clothes were an ongoing expense her first two years on the job.
Transportation and lunches	\$158	Sally tried to limit lunches and coffee breaks to \$4 per day more than home costs. She drove their second car to work, which cost 21 cents per mile.
Timesavers	\$240	To keep their sanity, Sally and Brad hired a housecleaning service at \$10 per hour, three hours a week, and bought a dishwasher. They also spent more on convenience foods and disposable diapers than before Sally went back to work.
Rushed shopping	\$175	Brad and Sally made a lot of hurried, unwise purchases. Sally also gave up shopping garage sales, formerly one of her big money savers and sources of enjoyment.
Rewards	\$100	Brad and Sally went out to eat and to the movies more often to reward themselves

		for all the upheaval. They also treated the kids to more junk food and toys.
Federal income tax	$160	Brad and Sally *over*estimated federal income tax.
State income tax	$75	They forgot about state tax.
Social Security	$128	They forgot about Social Security tax.
Deductible job expenses	$50	Sally spent $600 ($600 ÷ 12 months = $50 per month) her first year on professional dues, license renewal, and continuing education. She and Brad did not meet guidelines to claim these expenses as tax deductions and therefore paid the total cost.
Perks	$67	Employee benefits can sometimes *cost* money. Sally didn't know that 4 percent of her salary would be deducted for a retirement plan. She wasn't sure she'd live till retirement.
And what else?	$47	Sally used to write to Brad's parents once a week. After she returned to work, she often got too busy to write and spent more money on long-distance calls. She also spent extra on weight-control measures after her doughnut-coffee breaks added fifteen pounds in one year.
The bottom line	–$200	Sally's job-related expenses totaled $1,867. Her gross pay per month was $1,667. Her spendable income was –$200 ($1,667 – $1,867).

The above expenses left Sally working for LESS THAN NOTHING (–$200 per month). With Sally's true spendable income revealed, the $500 per month deficit is not so mysterious. The $200 deficit and the larger mortgage of $300 accounted for the $500 shortage per month (–$300 and –$200 = –$500).

They have joint custody of the children.

1

Child Care

When both parents plan to work outside the home, the first expense they're likely to consider is the cost of child care. Actually, taxes and other expenses may be larger, as shown in later chapters. But child-care costs—the cost of adult supervision of the kids, not the costs of food, clothing, shelter, and Nintendo—get first-chapter priority because so many second incomers believe their paychecks will be theirs to spend when the kids no longer need sitting, and they can't think of much else until child care is addressed.

This is not to discount child-care costs. They're *big.* You may have to spend even more on child care than those dreaded college bills. Of course, child care won't cost more than college if your children choose Ivy League schools. Likewise, if you plan to rely on amenable relatives or the latchkey solution. But realize there has never been a child who

1. Worked her way through day care.
2. Won a day-care scholarship for best finger painting.
3. Flunked out of day care.
4. Dropped out of day care to get married and/or find herself.
5. Received a student loan to cover day-care cost.

There are many reasons college bills may never materialize. Yet cost of child care is a here-and-now expense for two-income couples with young children, and sometimes their largest job-related expense. Grandma and Grandpa and the latchkey solution are the only defenses most working couples have against intolerable child-care costs. Finding a grandparent to charm is the problem. Chances are Grandma and Grandpa also have jobs, live five hundred miles away, or as they rightfully note, have paid their burpy-baby and terrible-twos' dues.

So, most working couples with young children pay large chunks of their income for child care. Care for one child usually costs *at least* $3,000 per year at a day-care center. Or it can cost more than $20,000 for a come-to-the-home nanny in a metropolitan area. Not surprising, prices run higher in major cities than rural areas. Prestigious names, expensive fixtures, and high costs, however, do not always mean quality care. The Royalty Day-Care Center, which charges twice the rate of the Bourgeois Center down the hill, may handle children like cattle on a freight train. Choosing good day care for the price you can afford is as complicated as selecting the right college.

Because their combined incomes were $120,000, Marcy and Rich thought they could afford a come-to-the-home nanny. They considered the $11,000-per-year cost a small price to pay, especially when contemplating their other options: an organized day-care center which charged $5,200 or a caregiver in a private home who charged $3,500. Since both of these alternatives involved a scramble to dress, feed, and drop off their sleepy daughter every morning, the nanny seemed a hands-down choice. Surprisingly, though, even substantial incomes can be eaten up by child-care and other job expenses.

Whether they could afford the nanny's price, however, turned out not to be an issue when Rich decided to take a leave of absence from his job as a quality control manager with an auto manufacturer. He was sure, if he just had more time, that he could improve the robot manipulative sensors used for delicate and precision assembly operations on automated production lines. There was no way he could concentrate with his daughter under the same roof (nanny or not). So, to guarantee peace for Rich (and save money when they cut back to one income), Marcy and Rich later chose the private home caregiver.

If you're not careful, Uncle Sam's smoke and mirrors can convince you that your child-care expense is reduced by his child-care credits and deductions. When you read chapter 7, Federal Income Tax, you'll notice

Brad and Sally received a $960 tax credit for child-care expenses, which was *subtracted from their taxes.* Brad and Sally recognized their tax savings, but later, they also thought of their child-care costs as reduced by the same credit. *Don't be fooled into subtracting the value of tax credits or deductions twice.* Child-care tax credits and deductions subtract from taxes, not child-care expense.

ADD IT UP

Because tax savings for child care are reflected in chapter 7, Federal Income Tax, and chapter 8, State Income Tax, calculating the child-care JRE here is a quick deal. *To find your average monthly child-care JRE, divide your annual expense by* 12 (*months*). (Be sure to use *annual* cost divided by 12. Otherwise, vacations, holidays, and months of unequal length will result in an inaccurate average monthly cost.)

Brad and Sally paid the day-care center $130 a week for fifty weeks ($130 × 50) for a total annual expense of $6,500.

BRAD AND SALLY'S CHILD-CARE EXPENSE

$6,500	÷	12	=	$542
Annual child-care cost				Monthly child-care JRE

YOUR CHILD-CARE EXPENSE

$_____	÷	12	=	$_____*
annual child-care cost				monthly child-care JRE

* ENTER this number as a negative on the child-care row on Your Second-Income JREs worksheet, pages 12–13.

That seemed too easy, and maybe it was. If you have no idea how your tax preparer figured your child-care credit or deduction, be sure to read chapter 7, postscript #2, Child-Care Tax Benefits.

2

PERSONAL UPKEEP

DOLLARS SPENT MAKING your on-the-job appearance acceptable are personal-upkeep job-related expenses. Examples of personal-upkeep expense can include cost of clothing, accessories, eyeglasses, shoes, dry cleaning, hairdos, manicures, facials, weight loss, and even face-lifts. Practically any exotic surgery, device, or service you buy to improve your appearance may be a personal-upkeep JRE *if* it is necessary to keep or advance in your job. Consequently, even liposuction could be a JRE for a ballet dancer, but never for a kindergarten teacher.

This chapter offers a great amount of room for number tinkering. Facing up to how much we spend on our physical image can be a soul-stirring experience that is easily abandoned when numbers approach those of the mortgage payment. Yet keep in mind, *everyone* spends to improve or make acceptable his or her appearance. Prejob expenses are not included in personal-upkeep JREs, making calculations slightly less painful (and less revealing).

Sally was a sweatshirt-and-jeans person before going back to work. But she wasn't a drudge either, and she also spent money on hair appointments and a basic wardrobe, some of which was appropriate for work. Thus, her personal-upkeep JRE was a low $125 per month. Nonetheless, she had to work at this number by including a lot of Wal-Mart specials in her work wardrobe. Sally spent over $125 per month on her appearance but included only expenses that stemmed from her job in her JRE list.

A second income often leads to spending more on nonwork apparel such as sports and evening wear. A reporter covering a presidential inaugural ball can count an evening gown or tuxedo as a JRE. Most of us, however, must either classify such purchases as financial goals (page 14) or rewards (chapter 6), and hope our incomes hold up to their cost.

To identify personal-upkeep JREs accurately, ask yourself: IS THIS PURCHASE A PREWORK EXPENSE, FINANCIAL GOAL, OR REWARD—OR IS IT A PURCHASE NECESSARY FOR ME TO KEEP OR ADVANCE IN MY JOB?

Friends of Brad and Sally counted the husband's income as their second paycheck because the wife's income was larger than his. He ran a financial consultant service from his home office for ten years and spent most of his work hours in Levi's and T-shirts. When he decided to take a better-paying downtown banking job, he was disappointed to find that a closet full of suits, ties, shoes, and dress shirts would eat up a large part of his additional income.

NOTE: Safety shoes and glasses, hard hats, uniforms, and some work clothes not suitable for everyday use are usually tax-deductible and should be listed in chapter 10, Deductible Job Expenses. Do not include them in this chapter.

CLOTHES

This JRE listing includes business suits, dresses, slacks, jeans, sweaters, shirts, blouses, jackets, coats, rain gear, headwear, and footwear. Any article of clothing that you need to work in or to get to and from work is a JRE; unless, of course, it is a financial goal or a prework expense, something you would have purchased regardless of your job. Include even the cost of a new girdle, if you need it to get into a certain work outfit, or the thermal underwear you need to work outside in a cold climate.

cathy® by Cathy Guisewite

Most undergarments, however, shouldn't be included because you'd be buying and wearing them anyway (we hope)!

There are no strict guidelines for identifying clothing JREs. We all need clothes, job or no job, making the separation of prework expense and JREs tedious. To help identify work-related clothes, ask yourself: IS THIS PURCHASE A PREWORK EXPENSE, FINANCIAL GOAL, OR REWARD—OR IS IT A PURCHASE NECESSARY FOR ME TO KEEP OR ADVANCE IN MY JOB?

There will be haunting gray areas. If you buy ten business suits for work but occasionally wear one suit off-hours, how do you classify their cost? If the suits average $200 each, you might say you have an annual JRE of $2,000 ($200 × 10). If this makes you feel as though you're shoplifting from your own closet, you may want to prorate costs between business and nonbusiness use and perhaps count the cost of only nine suits as a JRE.

Pantyhose Can "Run" a Budget

Hosiery deserves special mention because it requires constant replacement. It's possible to spend $15 per week on pantyhose if you prefer the finer brands at $7.50 per pair and must replace two pairs per week. Consider, $15 per week × 4 weeks per month = $60 per month pantyhose JRE!

Most women buy grocery-store pantyhose and make them last through several wearings. At any rate, hosiery can add many dollars to clothing JREs and shouldn't be forgotten.

Win, Lose, or "Tie" with Accessories

Floral or striped? Wide or narrow? Ties—and for that matter, most accessories—change fashion as surely as winter turns to spring. List as JREs the accessories that you need to complete the au courant look critical to your job: ties, belts, scarves, jewelry (including watches), socks, purses, and even the luggage you need for business trips—and the leather briefcase. If you're just following the winds of fashion and these purchases aren't work related, you'll need to account differently.

Stay Sane—Estimate!

Tallying clothing dollars according to separate uses can be frustrating and time-consuming. Don't get too bogged down with the proper classification of every scarf and shoelace. *Estimating* your *extra* clothing expense is good enough to get you through one year of work. If ten business suits will do it, divide their total estimated cost by 12 (months) for your monthly JRE. Next year you may want to spend money on only five new outfits yet need to buy a more stylish coat, some comfortable dress shoes, and replace your worn briefcase. Clothing JREs will fluctuate from year to year, but estimating on an annual basis will save a lot of number juggling. Don't anguish too long over these numbers. Still, be as accurate (and honest) as possible; it's your money.

NOTE: You may not think it's fair to charge all initial personal-upkeep cost to the first year on the job when later years may prove to be less expensive. But spreading cost over, say, a three-year period can be a bookkeeping nightmare. Can you keep track, for instance, of the gray suit, remembering you bought it in 1998? Will you remember to apportion its cost over 1998, 1999, and 2000, and finally drop it from the JRE list in 2001?

An extended schedule is also impractical because the life span of clothing is unpredictable. You may *think* the $500 coat will last a lifetime—well, at least three years. Then you tear it beyond repair when you snag a pocket on a door knob, or fashions change, or you sit on a freshly painted park bench.

When we take up in later chapters the costs for more reliable long-lived purchases, such as a dishwasher, it's still better to spread cost over just one year. Otherwise, your JRE chart will be skewed if you change jobs or number of hours worked, lose or quit your job, or forget to enter numbers from past years. Remember, though, that job expenses will vary from year to year, and it's therefore necessary to refigure JREs annually so you can recognize what your current expenses and spending habits are doing to your income.

THE EYES HAVE JRES

Eyeglasses are *not* normally JREs. However, if you need to keep a second pair in your desk at work because you would be job-disabled and unemployed if you lost or broke the first pair, the second pair's cost is a JRE. If contacts are necessary for your appearance at work, their cost is a JRE. Perhaps you believe your company favors a younger age bracket than you belong to, so you wear lineless bifocals (along with other age-saving tricks) to appear younger. The *extra* cost of your lineless bifocals is a JRE. Or maybe you work outside in the sun and a good pair of prescription sunglasses is important to doing your job well. (Of course, if your work requires safety glasses, their cost is not only a JRE but also probably tax-deductible and should be listed later in chapter 10, Deductible Job Expenses.)

MAINTENANCE AND SELF-IMPROVEMENT

Procedures and supplies needed for maintenance and self-improvement include hairdos and coloring, cosmetics and facials, manicures, eyebrow tweezing, weight-loss plans, face-lifts and other plastic surgery, exercise equipment, health club memberships, and so on. List even the sun-screen and poison ivy lotion you need because you work outside. Again, the key to identifying these expenses as personal-upkeep JREs is to ask yourself the big question: IS THIS PURCHASE A PREWORK EXPENSE, FINANCIAL GOAL, OR REWARD—OR IS IT A PURCHASE NECESSARY FOR ME TO KEEP OR ADVANCE IN MY JOB? Remember, on-the-job

CATHY ©1993 Cathy Guisewite. Reprinted with permission of UNIVERSAL PRESS SYNDICATE. All rights reserved.

appearance requirements are different for varying professions (e.g., ballet dancers and kindergarten teachers).

Before Sally returned to work, she wore her hair long and used a curling iron to add extra wave. She spent only $15 every three months for a trim (for an average cost of $5 per month). After she began working, she changed to a shorter style, which cost her $15 per month for a trim and $45 every three months for a permanent (average cost per month, $30). The difference in cost—$30 vs. $5—equals a $25-per-month JRE. The new style gave Sally a more professional appearance and was a quicker do, so she was able to get to work on time. If Sally decides to have her few gray hairs touched up or enroll in a weight-loss program, she shouldn't count these costs as JREs. Gray hair and extra pounds are professional handicaps for nightclub dancers, but not for social workers.

NOTE: In certain jobs, weight gain may be job-related but not a hindrance to keeping or advancing in your position (e.g., employees of Dunkin' Donuts and Baskin-Robbins; see chapter 12, And What Else?).

THE DRY CLEANER AND LAUNDRY SERVICE CAN CLEAN YOU OUT

Some people spend more on dry-cleaning bills than they do on the original cost of their clothing. It's possible to spend $1,200 or more per year on dry cleaning if you dress almost entirely in dry-clean-only clothing. For example, if you wear an average of four dry-clean-only outfits a week for fifty weeks at $6 each (4 × 50 × $6), you've spent $1,200!

Most people try to get at least two wearings out of each cleaning and avoid wearing nonwashable clothing so often. Sally was dollar smart and cut costs by buying only washable work clothing. But you can't throw business suits into the Maytag; for many readers, dry-cleaning bills will be notable JREs.

On the other hand, even though you buy washable work clothes, they may be impractical to clean at home. An auto mechanic may find greasy coveralls too much hassle to carry home and wash, especially since the clothes washer needs to be cleaned after the coveralls run through it. The cost of a laundry service is thus a personal-upkeep JRE (or the service can be listed later under timesavers, chapter 4).

ADD IT UP

Personal-upkeep JREs can rank between nothing and hundreds of dollars per month. If your appearance can make the difference in whether you keep or advance in your job, consider money spent an investment. Guilt trips are unnecessary here.

Sally's monthly personal-upkeep JREs follow. Fill in the worksheet below them with your own numbers. Remember to ask the big question before listing expenses as JREs: IS THIS PURCHASE A PREWORK EXPENSE, FINANCIAL GOAL, OR REWARD—OR IS IT A PURCHASE NECESSARY FOR ME TO KEEP OR ADVANCE IN MY JOB?

List the estimated average monthly cost of purchases necessary to keep or advance in your job. Do not include prejob expenses.

SALLY'S MONTHLY PERSONAL-UPKEEP EXPENSE ($)

	Personal-Upkeep JRE
Clothes, etc.	100
Accessories	0
Eyewear	0
Maintenance and self-improvement	25
Dry cleaning and laundry services	0
Other	0
Monthly personal-upkeep JRE	$125

YOUR MONTHLY PERSONAL-UPKEEP EXPENSE ($)

	Personal-Upkeep JRE
Clothes, etc.	____
Accessories	____
Eyewear	____
Maintenance and self-improvement	____
Dry cleaning and laundry services	____
Other	____
Monthly personal-upkeep JRE	$____★

★ ENTER this number as a negative on the personal-upkeep row on Your Second-Income JREs worksheet, pages 12–13.

3

Transportation, Lunches, and Coffee Breaks

It's not unusual for a worker to drive thirty miles (one way) to work, and to spend $6 per day on lunches and coffee breaks. The numbers sound innocent and hardly worth the mention. Yet they can easily cause job-related expenses of more than $400 per month!

Some people live within walking distance of their jobs, such as the waitress in the introduction. She walked to the restaurant where she worked, and the restaurant provided free coffee and meals to employees during work hours. As a result, she had no transportation, lunch, or coffee-break JREs.

Most readers will find their costs fall between these two extremes.

Note: Travel, meals, or entertainment expenses as *part* of your job *may* be tax-deductible (see chapter 10, Deductible Job Expenses). Include in this chapter only *non*deductible expenses such as the cost of commuting (going to and from your regular workplace), delivering and picking up children at the sitter's, and meals and coffee breaks during regular or extra work hours.

TRANSPORTATION

The cost and time spent getting to and from work can be an elusive and exasperating financial drain. Movie stars who commute between the two coasts may be able to afford the cost of a long-distance commute. Even so, a short commute for the rest of us may seriously damage the true value of our paychecks, even if we get the "bargain" rate on a monthly mass-transit commuting pass or partial reimbursement from our employers. Costs are often intangible and hard to identify, especially for commuters driving their own vehicles.

Mass-Transit Commuters

Transportation costs are quick to figure if you commute by mass transit. Workdays per month vary due to length of month, holidays, vacation, and sick time. Therefore, use annual cost of rides divided by 12 (months) to determine average monthly cost. The calculation is even easier if you buy a monthly commuting pass. Don't forget to subtract the cost of any employee reimbursement. Use the form on page 36, "Transportation JRE (for mass-transit commuters)," to figure your cost.

Personal-Vehicle Commuters

If you drive your own vehicle, transportation costs become muddled. Commuters often count only gasoline

TRANSPORTATION JRE

(for mass-transit commuters)

$_____ ×	______ =	$_____ ÷ 12 =	$_____ ★
Ride cost/day	Workdays /year	Annual trans. cost	Monthly trans. JRE

★ ENTER this number on Your Monthly Transportation, Lunch, and Coffee Break JRE form, page 47. Begin reading again on page 43, Lunches and Coffee Breaks.

and parking expense and neglect to include the more obscure costs such as maintenance, repairs, insurance, and depreciation.

The more commuting miles you drive, the more consequential cost per mile becomes when figuring transportation cost. One hundred miles per month at 20 cents per mile (100 × $.20) amounts to $20; at 30 cents per mile (100 × $.30), $30. A $10 difference in cost per month isn't worth worrying over too much. But 2,000 miles per month and the same 10-cent difference in cost per mile amounts to a $200 increase in cost (2,000 × $.20 = $400; 2,000 × $.30 = $600). Thus, the more commuting miles you drive, the more care you should take in determining your car's exact cost per mile.

For Less than Ten Miles per Day

The Internal Revenue Service allowed a standard mileage rate of 31.5 cents per mile for business purposes for 1997. Inasmuch as the IRS isn't known for handouts, it probably costs at least this much to drive the average vehicle. Although commuting costs are not deductible expenses, use 31.5 cents per mile to figure your transportation JRE if you drive less than ten miles a day to and from work. The result will be accurate enough and will save you the trouble of figuring your exact cost per mile. Multiply *annual* commuting miles (plus miles driven delivering and picking up children at the sitter's) by 31.5 cents. Add to this number the annual cost of parking and tolls; then divide by 12 (months) for monthly cost. Be sure to begin with annual numbers because workdays per month vary due to length of month, holidays, vacation, and sick time. In the following example, a commuter drove five miles per day, 240 working days per year (5 × 240 = 1,200 miles per year) and had a parking expense of one dollar per day.

TRANSPORTATION JRE

(for commuter driving less than ten miles per day)

1,200	× $.315 +	$240	= $618	÷ 12 =	$52
Annual commuting mileage	Cost per mile	Annual parking and toll cost	Annual cost		Monthly trans. JRE

YOUR TRANSPORTATION JRE

(for commuters driving less than ten miles per day)

_____	× $.315 +	$_____	= $_____	÷ 12 =	$_____ ⋆
Annual commuting mileage	Cost per mile	Annual parking and toll cost	Annual cost		Monthly trans. JRE

⋆ ENTER this number on Your Monthly Transportation, Lunch, and Coffee-Break JRE form, page 47. Begin reading again on page 43, Lunches and Coffee Breaks.

For More than Ten Miles per Day

Differences from the IRS's 31.5-cent-per-mile rate can result in substantial decreases or increases in your transportation JRE. So if you drive more than ten miles per day, figure your exact cost per mile carefully. The Vehicle Cost per Mile chart (on page 39) illustrates likely cost per mile for three new cars driven 75,000 miles over five years.

Cost per mile remains unchanged even if the vehicle is driven for reasons other than to get to and from work. If the $18,000 car on page 39 is used only 7,200 miles per year for commuting purposes (240 working days, 30 miles per day), and parking costs $1 per day, monthly transportation expense is figured as follows:

TRANSPORTATION JRE

(for commuter driving more than ten miles per day)

7,200	× $.36 +	$240	= $2,832	÷ 12 =	$236
Annual commuting mileage	Cost per mile	Annual parking and toll cost	Annual cost		Monthly trans. JRE

Obviously, your personal cost per mile can vary a great deal from the examples. You may buy a $10,000 car which gets 30 miles per gallon; insurance and property taxes will vary depending on where you live; maintenance and repairs are always rough estimates. And cost per mile is always subject to the vehicle's years of service and miles driven.

VEHICLE COST PER MILE

(based on 75,000 miles over five years) ($)

	Car 1	Car 2	Car 3
Cost of vehicle*	$12,000	$18,000	$24,000
Estimated resale value	–4,000	–6,000	–8,000
Loan interest**	2,639	3,958	5,277
Gasoline†	3,000	3,000	3,000
Insurance (5 years)	3,000	3,750	4,500
Property tax and license tags (five years)	1,200	1,800	2,400
Maintenance‡	2,350	2,350	2,350
Repairs§	500	500	500
Total cost	$20,689	$27,358	$34,027
Cost per mile§§	28 cents	36 cents	45 cents

* Includes sales tax, destination charges.
** Based on five-year loan, 10 percent interest, 20 percent down payment.
† 75,000 miles, 25 mpg, $1 per gallon (75,000 ÷ 25 × $1).
‡ Estimated five years' maintenance: $100 per year, wash and wax = $500; 25 oil changes at $25 each = $625; one set of tires at $300; one muffler, $90; one tail pipe, $85; two tune-ups at $150 each = $300; brake pads and shoes, $225; miscellaneous, $225.
§ An unpredictable number. After warranty expires, costs can vary between nothing and thousands of dollars.
§§ Divide total cost by expected miles (75,000 miles in above examples).

Porsches, Jags, and Other Dreams

It's true, some occupations almost demand the display of a well-to-do lifestyle. If a lawyer drives a rusty ten-year-old station wagon, most prospective clients will question his or her competence, based on apparent income. On the other hand, driving a new Porsche might raise questions about a lawyer's integrity or suggest an attitude of frivolity. A tactful compromise must be met. We can all count commuting cost per mile of a reliable vehicle as a JRE. Yet some occupations may require more than just a reliable car to intimate past successes and gain the confidence of potential clientele.

In short, don't buy an $80,000 Porsche and then base your transportation JRE on its costs. You *might* use the Porsche's costs when calculating cost per mile *if* it is the only car that will provide you with the reliability you need and if it alone will project the proper image for your position. (Porsche dealers, but few others, qualify here.) It's more likely the Porsche is a financial goal (you'd better earn a lot!) or you're giving yourself a very big reward (see chapter 6). If you've already bought the Porsche, ask yourself if a $15,000 Honda would have been adequate for your needs—if so, use Honda numbers to find your (honest) job-connected transportation cost per mile. The Porsche's extra cost should then be listed as a financial goal on page 14 or as a reward in chapter 6.

Leases

Car leasing, rather than buying, is becoming a popular choice. Cost per mile is generally higher on a leased car than one you own. But for many drivers, the advantages of driving a new car—the lower down payment and monthly payments, the worry-free miles—are worth the additional cost. Cost per mile can be figured much the same as with a car you own. Add down payment, administrative fees, total of monthly payments, gasoline, insurance, taxes, license tags, maintenance (if not included in lease), and other costs; divide total by miles you expect to drive the car for cost per mile.

Jon, retired from the air force (the pension was his first income), and part-time salesman (his second income), drove his leased car 60 miles per day commuting to his job, 120 work days per year, at a cost of 40 cents per mile. Without his part-time job, he and his wife would have made do with only one car. 120 days × 60 miles = 7,200 annual commuting mileage × $.40 cost per mile = $2,880 annual cost ÷ 12 months = $240 monthly transportation JRE. The cost of commuting put a serious crimp in Jon's usable income.

Good Used Vehicles and Old Heaps

Cars older than the examples on page 39 *usually* offer savings in cost per mile, although a seesaw effect comes into play when figuring cost per mile. High repair bills on an old car can erase the savings of lower price, insurance, tax, and interest costs. Thus, cost per mile for older vehicles is sometimes disappointing. Shade-tree mechanics can beat these teeter-totter results, but the rest of us risk the chance of becoming some auto mechanic's best customer.

Almost every family has an "Uncle Billy" who tells stories about his pickup truck with 300,000 miles that never needs so much as a new battery. Uncle Billys usually don't have jobs they have to get to at a regular time and they get high driving time bombs. Try to ignore your Uncle Billy.

Sally and Brad tried to beat the odds with their nine-year-old second car. Four years before Sally returned to work they purchased the car (similar to the $18,000 car on page 39) for $6,000 when it was five years old and had 75,000 miles. They estimated they could drive it another 75,000 miles before it would be wasted and worthless. The car was their only car for three years, and Brad's commuting miles, several family trips, and day-to-day errands used up most of the car's remaining mileage. Sally used the last of the car's miles her first year back at work. She drove 3,600 miles commuting and transporting the kids to and from the sitter's (240 working days × 15 miles per day). The car was a break-down looking for a place (and it found a place several times). Even so, repair bills were reasonable, considering the car's mileage and age, until the end when its transmission gave out. (See Sally's Vehicle Cost per Mile worksheet, page 43.)

Recall, only 3,600 of the 75,000 miles on Sally's car were job-related. She had parking costs of 75 cents a day (240 working days) for annual parking costs of $180.

SALLY'S TRANSPORTATION JRE

3,600	× $.21 +	$180	= $936	÷ 12 =	$78
Annual commuting mileage	Cost per mile	Annual parking and toll cost	Annual cost		Monthly trans. JRE

Base your own cost-per-mile calculations on the expected miles and years you plan to drive your car.

SALLY'S VEHICLE COST PER MILE

(based on 75,000 miles over five years) ($)

Cost of car*	6,000
Estimated resale value	–100
Interest on car loan**	323
Gasoline†	3,750
Insurance (5 years, liability only)	1,000
Property tax and license tags (5 years)	600
Maintenance‡	2,900
Repairs§	1,000
Total cost	$15,473
Cost per mile§§	21 cents

* Includes sales tax.
** Based on two-year loan, 10 percent interest, 50 percent down payment.
† As the car aged, it got fewer miles per gallon. 75,000 miles, 20 mpg, $1 per gallon (75,000 ÷ 20 × $1).
‡ Five years' maintenance: $100 per year, wash and wax = $500; 25 oil changes at $25 each = $625; two sets of tires, $600; one muffler, $90; one tail pipe, $85; three tune-ups at $150 each = $450; brake pads and shoes, $225; miscellaneous, $325.
§ Includes towing charges. Brad was not a shade-tree mechanic.
§§ Divide total cost by expected miles (75,000 in this example).

Remember, to find cost per mile, divide total cost by expected miles. (Use the worksheets on page 44.)

LUNCHES AND COFFEE BREAKS

Meal and coffee-break expenses (above and beyond at-home costs) during work hours are JREs. Although one day's expenses may sound quite harmless, a month's

YOUR VEHICLE COST PER MILE

(based on ______ miles, over ______ years)

Cost of car	______
Estimated resale value	– ______
Interest on car loan	______
Gasoline	______
Insurance	______
Property tax and license tags	______
Maintenance	______
Repairs	______
Total cost	$______
Cost per mile	______ cents*

* ENTER cost per mile on Your Transportation JRE form below.

YOUR TRANSPORTATION JRE

(for commuters driving more than ten miles per day)

______	× ______ +	$______	= $______	÷ 12 = $______ *
Annual commuting mileage	Cost per mile	Annual parking and toll cost	Annual cost	Monthly trans. JRE

* ENTER this number on Your Monthly Transportation, Lunch, and Coffee-Break JRE form, page 47.

total can prove to be a significant expense. Espresso bar triple grande cafe mochas and gourmet lunches can simultaneously expand your waistline and mangle your budget.

At-home expense can be practically nil. This is especially true if lunch consists of the leftovers that otherwise would be dumped or fed to the dog. And coffee made at home can cost less than two cents a cup. Of course, if you take a sandwich and coffee thermos to work, extra cost is minimal.

Betsy is too hassled in the mornings getting the kids ready for the babysitter to grab breakfast, so she stops at the deli next to her office in New York City, where coffee, juice, and a low-fat muffin cost $3. A typical deli sandwich and beverage at lunch cost her $5. A caffe latte at the trendy coffee bar during her mid-afternoon break is $1.50. That's $9.50 a day for breakfast, lunch, and coffee: a $190 JRE!

Sally was more conservative than Betsy and usually ate fast-food or vending-machine lunches, which averaged $3 per day more than she spent at home. She also spent an average of $1 per day on snacks and coffee.

cathy® **by Cathy Guisewite**

SALLY'S LUNCH AND COFFEE-BREAK EXPENSE

$3	+	$1	×	240	=	$960	÷ 12 =	$80
Lunch cost per day		Coffee-break cost per day		Working days per yr.		Cost per yr.		Monthly JRE

YOUR LUNCH AND COFFEE-BREAK EXPENSE

$_____	+	$_____	×	_____	=	$_____	÷ 12 =	$_____★
Lunch cost per day		Coffee-break cost per day		Working days per yr.		Cost per yr.		Monthly JRE

★ ENTER this number on Your Monthly Transportation, Lunch, and Coffee-Break JRE form, page 47.

ADD IT UP

Transportation, lunch, and coffee-break costs are easy to overlook and underrate because they are often paid in cash. Simple changes, such as joining a car pool and carrying a bag lunch from home, can make a big difference in a paycheck's spending power.

After Sally's example on the next page, add your transportation JRE (from page 36, 37, or 44) to your lunch and coffee-break JRE (above).

SALLY'S MONTHLY TRANSPORTATION, LUNCH, AND COFFEE-BREAK JRE

$78	+	$80	=	$158
Monthly transportation JRE		Monthly lunch and break JRE		Monthly transportation, lunch, and break JRE

YOUR MONTHLY TRANSPORTATION, LUNCH, AND COFFEE-BREAK JRE

$_____	+	$_____	=	$_____ *
Monthly transportation JRE		Monthly lunch and break JRE		Monthly transportation, lunch, and break JRE

* ENTER this number as a negative on the transportation and lunches row on Your Second-Income JREs worksheet, pages 12–13.

* * *

A frazzled working mother was asked if she needed to work outside the home.

"Oh, yes," she replied. "I have car payments, which I could never afford if I didn't work."

"Do you need such a nice car?"

"Of course," she retorted. "I need my car to get to work!"

4

TIMESAVERS

IF YOU WORK a full-time, forty-hour-per-week job, you have, in essence, "sold" forty hours of your time. Workers are, in effect, timesavers for employers or clientele, who haven't the time to learn or do the job themselves. Unfortunately, after selling forty hours of your time, you will probably find yourself racing the clock, and will also resort to using timesavers. Household timesavers come in many guises—housekeepers, dishwashers, disposable diapers—but they all have one common purpose, *to save time!*

A well-managed business, through layoffs and attrition, will never employ so many workers (i.e., timesavers) that it sacrifices profits; a well-managed household budget should adhere to the same guideline. Working for the green can be a futile effort if you exhaust your income on timesavers. If you scrutinize your expenses closely, you may find that your second paycheck goes largely to support the assortment of timesavers required so that you can "buy back" sold time. The circle can be unending and last a lifetime.

Modern technology threatens to consume our most precious possession—time. We are so dazzled by the array of labor-saving products available that we lose sight of the extra income (and hours) these products require to cover their costs. A parent can easily spend $1,000 a year on the disposable diapers* required by most day-care centers in order to work outside the home. Close analysis of job-related expenses may disclose the $1,000 to be a decisive subtraction from spendable income. You might prefer to wash three loads of diapers per week rather than work a forty-hour week for someone else. A "time warp" can evolve if you work to pay for timesavers so that you have the time to work for someone else.

Julie, a part-time music teacher, worked just three hours a day and had summers and school holidays off. Because of her short hours, she spent nothing extra on timesavers. Yet her friend Sara, who worked full-time, went to extremes and spent $500 per month on these expenses. Julie and Sara illustrate how dollars spent on timesavers generally correspond to the number of hours worked outside the home. Full-time second incomers often find timesavers the last of the job expenses they are willing to cut—for they are what make the race with the

* Disposable diapers cost about 25 cents each. With only 12 changes per day, cost is $3 per day or (365 × $3) $1,095 per year.

clock winnable. On the other hand, a half-time worker may have no need for extra timesavers. Sally and Brad hired a housecleaner, but if one of them had been working part-time, that person might have had the time to do the cleaning, too.

Marcy and Rich (chapter 1) didn't realize how much they'd save on timesavers when they cut back to one income so Rich could stay home to work on a new design for robot sensors. Rich discovered he could only keep his creative juices flowing for about five hours a day before he needed a break. Some of his worst cases of "inventor's block" were cured while he vacuumed, dusted, did laundry, and cooked dinner. Often he could hardly remember where he'd cleaned because his mind returned to his robot problems while he vacuumed. So his time spent on household chores wasn't wasted, and Marcy and Rich no longer needed a housecleaning service, to eat out so often, or to buy so many convenience products.

A cautious compromise must be met, though, between the saving or spending of money on timesavers. It's possible to work harder and longer hours at home, as opposed to working a full-time job, if you cut back too far on timesavers.

WHO (AND WHAT) IS A TIMESAVER?

Three kinds of timesavers can be employed to stretch your hours:

- People
- Machines
- Convenience products

A timesaver is not necessarily a JRE. We all use timesavers, and their appropriateness isn't always initiated by lack of time because we're working full time. Great-grandma's scrub board and homemade lye soap are not the measuring points above which we establish all timesavers as JREs. A timesaver's cost is only a JRE if you need it to recapture time spent working for someone else. A clothes washer and dryer are certainly timesavers, but not necessarily JREs. If you would own a washer and dryer regardless of whether you worked, their cost does not stem from a job-created time deficit.

People

Multitudes of people out there are willing (for a price) to help with your time problems. And many will happily charge you more for one hour's work than you earn in an hour. Therefore, it's necessary to establish what you have the time *and ability* to do for yourself to avoid spending all your income on these services. Even so, avoid overrating your abilities or the jobs you would do for yourself if you were not working for someone else. If you count the chimney sweep's bill a JRE, be sure you have the ability to clean the chimney *and* would have done the job yourself if you'd had the time. Most of us will have to admit that the chimney sweep and most other repair, remodeling, and maintenance services are beyond our expertise or interests, and their costs are not

JREs. A people timesaver's cost is not a JRE unless you could have—and would have—done the job yourself had you not been double-shifting.

Years ago I spent one "hair-raising" evening a month cutting three squirming sons' hair. Later, the home barbershop was permanently shut down because of my inability to satisfy some very fussy customers. Job or no job, there were barber bills, so the haircut costs couldn't be counted as JREs.

Ambitious penny pinchers (I'm one of the best examples) often do away with people timesavers to the point of making themselves and others miserable. My husband, Jim, recalls the Winter of Our Discontent when I decided upholstering was an overvalued occupation. I invested a sizable sum in fabric to redo the living room. He spent most of the winter sitting in a beanbag chair, listening to my wails of despair. I can never count an upholsterer's bill a JRE.

A math teacher hires a tutor to help her fifth-grade son with fractions; a concert pianist pays someone to give her daughter piano lessons. These costs are JREs because they don't have *time* to teach their own children. *Or,* they may not be JREs if the teacher and pianist don't have the *ability* to teach their own kids. Children can be balky and uncooperative for their own parents—and industrious students for strangers. An expense isn't a JRE if you'd pay it even if you had forty-eight hour days.

The Yellow Pages are packed with people timesavers advertising their skills. Included are:

Accountants, bookkeepers, income tax preparers
Sewing and alterations services

- Repair, maintenance, and remodeling services
  - Auto mechanics and maintenance services
  - Plumbers
  - Roofers
  - Electric, heating, air-conditioning contractors
  - Appliance repair services
  - Painters
  - Wallpaperers
  - Swimming pool services
  - Dry wallers
  - Carpenters
  - Cabinetmakers
  - Upholsterers
  - Drapery makers
  - Interior decorators
- Housecleaners
  - Window washers
  - Carpet cleaners
  - Floor waxers
  - Chimney sweeps
- Pet groomers
- Barbers and beauticians
- Laundry and ironing services
- Yard care
  - Gardeners
  - Landscape designers, contractors
  - Mowing services
  - Snow removal services
- Shopping services
- Chauffeur and delivery services
- Caterers
- Cooks, chefs

Restaurants
Teachers, tutors

Your own kids can be people timesavers as well. If your teenager needs extra cash and you need extra help with the house and yard care, you may be able to strike a deal. Expect to spend time, though, on lengthy wage negotiations and frequent quality control inspections.

GOOD NEWS: If you have a child younger than thirteen years old, you *may* be able to include salaries paid to housekeepers and cooks with child-care expense for a tax credit or deduction. The service, of course, must at least partly benefit the child. As with child care, these tax credits and deductions affect taxes owed—not the household help cost listed in this chapter. (See chapter 7, postscript #2, Child-Care Tax Benefits.)

We all have different skills. Some of us can and do fix our own leaky faucets, change the oil in the car, repaint the house, mow the lawn, cater our daughters' wedding receptions, or do our own taxes. The costs of these services are not JREs, however, unless you can and would do them yourself, except for the time shortage brought about by your second income.

Machines

One hundred years ago timesaving household machines were in short supply. Today, we're caught up in a tangle of electric cords, time-payment plans, utility bills, and service contracts. Up-to-date automation has so invaded our thinking and standard of living that we feel deprived unless we have it all.

Yet not all machines are timesavers, and even fewer are JREs. The garage-door opener or the garbage disposer, which each save a mere two minutes per day, hardly qualify as timesavers. The food processor may take more time to clean than it saves chopping. A self-cleaning oven sounds like a justified JRE. Yet unless you're a clean-oven fanatic, the garage-door opener may be a bigger timesaver! Nice-to-own does not qualify a machine or appliance as a timesaver. Many available gadgets take some of the drudgery out of life, but their contribution to the time bank is minimal.

Timesaving machines cannot automatically be classified as JREs. You shouldn't count the dishwasher you already own as a job expense when you take on an outside job. Likewise, replacement appliances aren't often legitimate JREs. A new clothes washer doesn't count as a JRE if you would have replaced your defunct one regardless of your double shift—or if you bought it to match the new wallpaper. A true machine timesaver JRE is purchased so that your hours will stretch to accommodate a double shift.

Dishwashers, clothes washers, dryers, and microwave ovens are all timesavers that can qualify as JREs. Their help with the clock race is obvious. A less apparent electric helper is the refrigerator-freezer. A large refrigerator-freezer, or separate freezer, may add hours to your days by saving on grocery shopping and cooking time. Time-consuming grocery shopping can be cut to

Calvin and Hobbes **by Bill Watterson**

the minimum if you have adequate refrigerator-freezer space. And when making a favorite dish, it takes only a few extra minutes to double or triple the recipe and freeze the extra. Count as a JRE the *difference* in cost between the appliance you'd own without an outside job and the larger or better one you buy because of your job.

A variety of home office timesavers can make life easier and the hours go further too. Some may help out with home chores, others with work you bring home from the office. (Check tax rules: some may be tax-deductible and should be listed with Deductible Job Expenses, chapter 10.)

Heading the list of home office timesavers are: computers; printers; software, including money management and tax preparation programs; and fax machines. An electronic notebook and a copy machine may also be counted as timesavers.

A home phone can't be counted as a JRE because you'd surely have one whether you work or not. But there are telephone extras that make your phone time, and the rest of your life, more productive. Some phone accessories that may be job-related include the cost of an answering machine, a pager and paging service, and Call Forwarding, Call Waiting, Call Blocker, Call Return, and Caller ID. Also, don't forget the cost of a cellular phone, which makes it possible for you to make personal and business calls during the usually wasted time you spend commuting to and from work.

Lawn and garden hobbyists will discover many of their best machine timesavers are located in the garage or yard. One couple found a riding lawn mower, gas-powered trimmer, and automatic watering system essential to stretch their hours so that they could each work full-time. Timesaving JREs will show up in diverse places, depending on your interests. So the ranking of machines and electric appliances as timesaving JREs is a personal investigation.

Convenience Products

Your great-grandparents would have called store-bought bread, butter, and jelly "convenience foods," if they'd ever heard such a term. Likewise, neither had ever heard of disposable products. My mother-in-law, a depression-era mom, recalls considering the third cloth diaper a luxury. She had one on the baby, one on the line, and one for emergencies! At the time, she would have thought disposable diapers an outrageous waste.

The definition of ready-made goods has changed over the decades, and even yet, each of us has different ideas on what is a bare-bones product. Great-great-grandma may have thought milled flour to make an apple pie a "convenience." Now, an apple pie can be:

- Made completely from scratch (but with milled flour)
- Made with a ready-made crust
- Made with a ready-made filling
- Made with both ready-made crust and filling
- Purchased completely ready-made

Not all convenience products should be counted JREs. If you've never made a pie in your life, don't count the extra cost of ready-made pies as a JRE. A pre-work timesaver isn't a JRE because its cost does not originate from a job-created time shortage. A quick glance at your grocery cart will reveal most of the extra ready-made and disposable products you buy due to double-shifting. If you formerly made potato salad from scratch but now see deli potato salad in the cart, the *difference* in cost is a JRE.

Some ready-made products are cheaper than scratch products. It's much more expensive to make lemonade and orange juice from scratch than from a concentrate mix. Likewise for some soups, breads, and Hamburger-Helper-type box dinners. When the total cost of equipment, supplies, and fuel is considered, home-prepared foods are usually but not always cost-effective. Some traditionalists boast about dollars saved baking bread, canning homegrown vegetables . . . With packaged yeast alone costing as much as 40 cents for one loaf of bread and canning lids 10 cents each, such claims don't always add up. It's always wise to do the calculations.

Notice that convenience products aren't limited to the grocery store. Ready-made clothing can be an extra job expense for a former home seamstress. Nevertheless, fabric and sewing notions aren't cheap, and it's very easy to overestimate the difference in costs between homemade and ready-made outfits. Many home sewers would do better to watch for good sales on ready-made clothing, or investigate thrift stores and garage sales. It's also disappointing to a home seamstress to discover she's invested time and money in a creation that adds an illusionary twenty pounds to her weight. A ready-made dress would have revealed this secret in the fitting room and saved a costly mistake.

Convenience products are everywhere and invade the budget in unexpected places. The premixed yard and garden spray as well as the deli salad can be classified JREs. Your former and present do-it-yourself disposition determines if a convenience product is a JRE.

ADD IT UP

Sally and Brad hired a housecleaner for three hours per week for 48 weeks at $10 per hour ($10 × 3 [hours] × 48 [weeks] = $1,440 ÷ 12 [months] = $120 per month JRE). They bought a dishwasher ($360 ÷ 12 [months] = $30 per month JRE). Their one-year-old wore disposable diapers most of the time at an extra cost of $60 per month, and Sally and Brad estimated they spent $30 more per month on convenience foods than before Sally returned to work. (One stroll past the grocery deli can blow a twenty-dollar bill, so they did well in this category.)

BRAD AND SALLY'S MONTHLY TIMESAVER EXPENSE ($)

People:	
Housecleaning	–120
Restaurant meals	____
Yard care	____
Repairs, maintenance	____
Other	____
Machines:*	
Dishwasher	–30
Microwave oven	____
Washer/dryer	____
Refrigerator	____
Freezer	____
Office, telephone equipment	____
Lawn, garden equipment	____
Other	____
Convenience products:	
Disposable diapers	–60
Convenience foods	–30
Clothing	____
Other	____
Total monthly JRE	–$240

* Divide cost by 12 (months).

Closely analyze your timesaver JRE profile. You may find that timesavers aren't the reason you have *time* to work, but the reason you *must* work.

YOUR MONTHLY TIMESAVER EXPENSE

People:	
Housecleaning	_____
Restaurant meals	_____
Yard care	_____
Repairs, maintenance	_____
Other	_____
Machines:*	
Dishwasher	_____
Microwave oven	_____
Washer/dryer	_____
Refrigerator	_____
Freezer	_____
Office, telephone equipment	_____
Lawn, garden equipment	_____
Other	_____
Convenience products:	
Disposable diapers	_____
Convenience foods	_____
Clothing	_____
Other	_____
Total Monthly JRE	$_____**

NOTE: List estimated average monthly cost of purchases necessary because of a time shortage created by a second income. Don't include prework timesavers or financial goals.

* Divide cost by 12 (months).

** ENTER this number as a negative on the timesavers row on Your Second-Income JREs worksheet, pages 12–13.

5

Rushed Shopping

THE TWO-INCOME family trades time for dollars and, in return, is left short of the time necessary to spend their hard-earned dollars carefully. Hence, an often overlooked and indistinct job expense arises: the cost of rushed and thoughtless shopping. The old saying "It's not how much you make, but how much you keep" is a personal directive for two-income couples.

Careful comparison shopping is the axis upon which a well-managed budget turns. It is the sometimes laborious and time-consuming task of cautiously weighing the available choices. Often comparison shopping results in the decision to spend elsewhere, to spend on a different item, or (the bane of business) not to spend at all.

It is, therefore, no wonder that businesses will go to no end to confuse customers and encourage impulse buying at every turn. Insurance companies, with legal jargon and fine print, make policy comparisons exasperating. Appliance dealers have even been known to change model numbers on national brand items to make price comparisons difficult. Grocery store chains are leaders in price camouflage with a yo-yo system that keeps prices moving up and down so fast it's nearly impossible to identify the cheapest store. To be known for best value, grocery stores advertise sale items, while raising prices on other purchases you're bound to buy if they can get you inside their doors. You may make a special trip to buy lettuce at a bargain price, only to find the savings wiped out by a higher price on the Roquefort salad dressing you want. A successful shopper views this chicanery as a challenging, yet time-consuming, mind game.

Careful comparison shoppers outsmart not only the businesses they buy from, but also Uncle Sam. Uncle Sam will tax it if he can find it, but he'll never find the dollars you save comparison shopping! If you are in the 50 percent tax bracket (federal, state, plus Social Security) you must earn two dollars for every one dollar you bring home. Work one hour, earn (for instance) twenty dollars, keep ten dollars. Or—comparison-shop one hour, save twenty dollars, keep twenty dollars! "A penny saved is a penny earned" may have been true in Ben Franklin's day, but with today's taxes, a penny saved can be worth two earned.

How much you can lose due to rushed shopping depends a lot on your income. If you have a large income, you are likely to have more opportunities to spend (and waste money by not comparison shopping) than someone with a small income. If Donald Trump doesn't take time to shop around, he can lose more money by missing a 10 percent off yacht deal than you can by missing a bargain-priced used bass boat at a garage sale. Even though you lose 20 percent of your total income through careless shopping, your losses will not be as high as those of a millionaire who wastes the same 20 percent. In short, the larger your income, the higher your rushed shopping JRE will be if neither partner has time to study financial decisions carefully.

The Second-Income Job-Related Expenses chart on pages 10–11 shows that even Best examples in every income bracket can expect to lose $100 a month because of rushed shopping. Although the financial leaks caused by hurried buying are usually invisible, they can squeeze $100 out of a monthly budget in the grocery store alone. Plus, as income rises, the probability for loss increases. You can easily lose $300 per month to rushed shopping, as the $52,000 Typical example demonstrates. If you don't pinpoint the root of these losses, you'll blow your monthly budget and wonder why there's so much month left at the end of your money!

COMPARISON-SHOP FOR *EVERYTHING*

You can comparison-shop for almost anything you spend money on. Even monopolistic utilities may offer some respite in the form of different rate and payment schedules based on consumption and peak-load hours. There are no tax stores that sell taxes at bargain rates, but studying tax laws is a means of comparison shopping for cheaper taxes. Thus, items you can shop for include:

Automobiles, transportation
Bank and credit card fees
Clothing, jewelry, and other personal-upkeep expenses (see chapter 2)
Entertainment, recreation, vacations
Furniture
Gasoline
Gifts
Groceries
Health care (medical, dental, eye, prescription drugs)
Housing
Household appliances
Insurance (all kinds)
Interest rates on loans, including credit cards
Investments, retirement plans
Taxes
Timesavers (see chapter 4)
Utilities (gas, electric, telephone)

Time may seem as well spent shopping to save $100 on a month's groceries as the time spent shopping interest rates to save $100 on the mortgage payment. Yet the effort and time expended to save $100 on groceries must be duplicated monthly; a reduced interest rate will save monthly, with no additional effort, for as long as the next thirty years!

"Cathys" spend their lives running from one end of the mall to the other. Unfortunately, the most profitable

cathy® **by Cathy Guisewite**

shopping usually requires brain power rather than shoe leather. After a stressful day at the office, walking the mall may be a means of unwinding. Some people always find time and energy to shop for clothes, but will put off investigating ways to save on their auto insurance until they're eligible for the AARP plan. Truly gainful shopping often involves dull and irksome subjects. On the other hand, cultivating the "thrill of the chase" to find the best buy can provide you with free entertainment!

Ideally, you should save both ways: on the clothes and on car insurance. Still, we're all limited by time and interests. Shopping for a new suit can be fun. Car insurance is tedious and uninteresting to most people, even though reduced premiums could render much larger savings than a suit on sale.

The shopping game is won not with gasoline dollars, tax dollars, clothing dollars, insurance dollars . . . , but with *total* dollars; how each of us chooses to save them may be quite individual. Shoe-leather shopping is a pawn in the shopping chess game, necessary, but not often decisive. The game's queen is brain-power shopping. Yet nothing is harder to do than study insurance, taxes, investments, or interest rates after a hectic day at the office. It's easier just to walk the mall one more time.

Assign Shopping Hours a Dollar Value

Cathy and her mother probably spent one hour returning the scarf and saved $3. If they shared the $3 savings, they each saved (or earned) $1.50 for their hour's work.

If, however, Cathy had spent four hours researching car insurance and calling agents for price quotes, she could have saved $100 per year or $400 over the remaining four years she plans to own her car. $400 ÷ 4 hours = $100 per hour.

I once spent a total of thirty hours studying life insurance and investments and discovered Jim and I could buy twice as much term life insurance as the whole life insurance we owned for half the money. The cash values of the whole life plans and saved premiums were invested in low-yield but safe investments that should easily clear $30,000 over the mature values of the whole life plans. $30,000 ÷ 30 hours = $1,000 per hour!

You don't necessarily have to keep detailed records of time spent and dollars saved. But do make informal mental notes of shopping hours' profits so that you know where your time is most wisely invested.

Shoe-Leather Shopping

Although shoe-leather shopping doesn't usually net the best returns per hour, it shouldn't be discounted either. One well-spent hour shopping the mall can net $20 or more. At one hour per week that's (52 × $20) $1,040 tax-free dollars per year. Many a dollar is lost from a lack of time to study and compare options thoroughly.

Unfortunately, shoe-leather shopping costs usually explode during the holiday season. An otherwise careful shopper can go berserk while in search of the perfect gifts, the perfect holiday trimmings, the perfect menu, the perfect New Year's outfit. . . . Probably the most common holiday prayer: "Please help me find it all!! (I'll worry about paying later.)"

A large part of shoe-leather shopping is done in grocery stores, but watch out for grocery store gurus who claim you can effortlessly cut your grocery bills in half with savvy shopping. Unrealistic expectations can be discouraging and may cause you to stop trying. A 50 percent savings is unlikely unless you're seriously dedicated or dieting and shoplifting on the side.

Comparison shopping by itself probably won't save half on your grocery bill. But you may be able to reach a 50 percent goal if you're willing to scale back on convenience and deli foods (see timesavers, chapter 4), eat hamburger instead of steak, use day-old bread, and cut expensive junk foods (see rewards, chapter 6).

Consider, if you are to save half on grocery bills through comparison shopping alone, you must manage, on average, to buy every item in your cart at half price. Using coupons (preferably double), reading labels, and comparing brands and package sizes will save some money. In addition, by stocking up on sale items, buying house brands, and joining a food co-op, you will be able to increase savings—but go too far with stocking up and your home will become a warehouse. Besides, many sale items are perishables; a three-month supply of lettuce would be food for the garbage disposal. And innumerable grocery items never go on sale at all. If you save 20 to 30 percent of your usual grocery bill through careful comparison shopping, you've done as well as anyone—except for the dieters and shoplifters.

Still, within limits, stocking up on sale items is a good technique for upping savings at the grocery store and the mall. If you keep only $100 ahead of your current needs, and buy and roll over $100 worth of merchandise on 30 percent–off sale items every month, the original $70 saves $30 per month or ($30 × 12) $360 a year. Wall Street's market doesn't deliver dividends like this. The trouble with the *grocery* market is that the investment limits are set by storage space and sale items you can use in a reasonable time. No one is going to get rich in the grocery market. Then again, no one's going to jump out a window because he or she bought canned green beans and later the price went down!

Interest Rates

You'll never outsmart the wheelers and dealers out to pick your pockets if you don't understand how interest rates affect loan payments and investments. Hours spent comparison shopping can be wasted if you ignore the force interest rates wield. Brad and Sally shopped till they dropped for the best house buy. They then wiped out the money they saved by failing to understand the significance of interest rates on their monthly loan payments.

Car dealers lure buyers intent on getting the best price with low prices linked to high interest loans, which they, of course, finance. Conversely, they reel in the buyers concentrating on interest rates, with low interest loans combined with high prices. They don't care whether they make their money off the car or the loan. I once encountered an interest-rate charlatan willing to let *me* name the price on a house *he* was selling. The catch turned out to be that as the price went down, the interest rate went up. (He, of course, wanted to finance the loan.) It's just as risky not understanding interest rate results as not knowing price!

Eighth-grade math teachers teach *I* = *PRT* (*I*nterest = *P*rincipal × *R*ate × *T*ime). If you understand this formula you can pass an eighth-grade math test—and that's about it! The formula only works for single-payment loans and uncompounded interest on investments. Most loans are paid by monthly installments, and investments are compounded monthly, quarterly, or semiannually, making interest calculations incredibly complicated.

Avoid the math. Amortization or mortgage payment tables come in books the size of pocket calculators and sell for around five dollars at most book stores. If you ask, your lender or real estate agent may even give you one. Armed with one of these books it's easy to figure the payments, interest, and loan progress on any size loan for periods ranging from one to forty years. Car loans, refrigerator loans, college loans, house loans, . . . can all be calculated with the tables. One glance at the tables (see example tables, pages 72–73) will illustrate how payments are affected by a change in interest rates or a shortened schedule. Most good comparison shoppers have one of these books and give them as gifts at weddings.

Other Recommended Reading

Most second incomers don't think they have the time to study money management and do careful comparison shopping. The study and saving of money require time, and a tight time schedule thus results in an invisible cost: rushed shopping job-related expense. Careless spending is sometimes the biggest drain on a second income. Careful spending can be the key to single-income survival.

There are thousands of books, magazines, newsletters, TV, and radio shows that explain how to make the best use of your dollars. Some will have you clipping grocery coupons; others, running the fast lane in the stock market. It's up to you to decide where your shopping time can most gainfully be invested. No set of rules is best for everyone, and no financial expert is infallible.

I recommend the following books as a beginning point. If you can get through them and still have wind in your sails, you probably have the aptitude for modern money management. Whether you begin with these books or others of your own choosing is not important. The point is to begin somewhere. And then, continue your education by reading works by reliable and current authors. When you see the same message repeated by several respected authorities, you'll know when it's time to listen. Investing the time *now* to learn how to manage your money will reap benefits for the rest of your life.

Penny Pinching, by Lee and Barbara Simmons (Bantam Books, 1996, $5.99). Brief and easy instructions on how to save on credit cards, prescription

Monthly Payment Loans 8.00%

Amortization Period in Years

	10	15	20	25	30
$ 100	1.22	0.96	0.84	0.78	0.74
200	2.43	1.92	1.68	1.55	1.47
300	3.64	2.87	2.51	2.32	2.21
400	4.86	3.83	3.35	3.09	2.94
500	6.07	4.78	4.19	3.86	3.67
600	7.28	5.74	5.02	4.64	4.41
700	8.50	6.69	5.86	5.41	5.14
800	9.71	7.65	6.70	6.18	5.88
900	10.92	8.61	7.53	6.95	6.61
1,000	12.14	9.56	8.37	7.72	7.34
2,000	24.27	19.12	16.73	15.44	14.68
3,000	36.40	28.67	25.10	23.16	22.02
4,000	48.54	38.23	33.46	30.88	29.36
5,000	60.67	47.79	41.83	38.60	36.69
6,000	72.80	57.34	50.19	46.31	44.03
7,000	84.93	66.90	58.56	54.03	51.37
8,000	97.07	76.46	66.92	61.75	58.71
9,000	109.20	86.01	75.28	69.47	66.04
10,000	121.33	95.57	83.65	77.19	73.38
15,000	182.00	143.35	125.47	115.78	110.07
20,000	242.66	191.14	167.29	154.37	146.76
25,000	303.32	238.92	209.12	192.96	183.45
30,000	363.99	286.70	250.94	231.55	220.13
35,000	424.65	334.48	292.76	270.14	256.82
40,000	485.32	382.27	334.58	308.73	293.51
45,000	545.98	430.05	376.40	347.32	330.20
50,000	606.64	477.83	418.23	385.91	366.89
55,000	667.31	525.61	460.05	424.50	403.58
60,000	727.97	573.40	501.87	463.09	440.26
65,000	788.63	621.18	543.69	501.69	476.95
70,000	849.30	668.96	585.51	540.28	513.64
75,000	909.96	716.74	627.34	578.87	550.33
80,000	970.63	764.53	669.16	617.46	587.02
85,000	1,031.29	812.31	710.98	656.05	623.70
90,000	1,091.95	860.09	752.80	694.64	660.39
95,000	1,152.62	907.87	794.62	733.23	697.08
100,000	1,213.28	955.66	836.45	771.82	733.77
110,000	1,334.61	1,051.22	920.09	849.00	807.15
120,000	1,455.94	1,146.79	1,003.73	926.18	880.52
125,000	1,516.60	1,194.57	1,045.56	964.78	917.21
130,000	1,577.26	1,242.35	1,087.38	1,003.37	953.90
140,000	1,698.59	1,337.92	1,171.02	1,080.55	1,027.28
150,000	1,819.92	1,433.48	1,254.67	1,157.73	1,100.65
160,000	1,941.25	1,529.05	1,338.31	1,234.91	1,174.03
170,000	2,062.57	1,624.61	1,421.95	1,312.09	1,247.40
175,000	2,123.24	1,672.40	1,463.78	1,350.68	1,284.09
180,000	2,183.90	1,720.18	1,505.60	1,389.27	1,320.78
190,000	2,305.23	1,815.74	1,589.24	1,466.46	1,394.16
200,000	2,426.56	1,911.31	1,672.89	1,543.64	1,467.53
220,000	2,669.21	2,102.44	1,840.17	1,698.00	1,614.29
225,000	2,729.88	2,150.22	1,882.00	1,736.59	1,650.98
230,000	2,790.54	2,198.00	1,923.82	1,775.18	1,687.66
240,000	2,911.87	2,293.57	2,007.46	1,852.36	1,761.04
$250,000	3,033.19	2,389.14	2,091.11	1,929.55	1,834.42

NOTE: Monthly payment of principal and interest for a $100,000 loan at 8 percent over thirty years is $733.77; at 11 percent, $952.33; at 8 percent over fifteen years, $955.66. Comparison shopping using these tables quickly shows how interest rate and time affect monthly payment and total outlay over the loan's lifetime.

Monthly Payment Loans 11.00%

Amortization Period in Years

	10	15	20	25	30
$ 100	1.38	1.14	1.04	0.99	0.96
200	2.76	2.28	2.07	1.97	1.91
300	4.14	3.41	3.10	2.95	2.86
400	5.52	4.55	4.13	3.93	3.81
500	6.89	5.69	5.17	4.91	4.77
600	8.27	6.82	6.20	5.89	5.72
700	9.65	7.96	7.23	6.87	6.67
800	11.03	9.10	8.26	7.85	7.62
900	12.40	10.23	9.29	8.83	8.58
1,000	13.78	11.37	10.33	9.81	9.53
2,000	27.56	22.74	20.65	19.61	19.05
3,000	41.33	34.10	30.97	29.41	28.57
4,000	55.11	45.47	41.29	39.21	38.10
5,000	68.88	56.83	51.61	49.01	47.62
6,000	82.66	68.20	61.94	58.81	57.14
7,000	96.43	79.57	72.26	68.61	66.67
8,000	110.21	90.93	82.58	78.41	76.19
9,000	123.98	102.30	92.90	88.22	85.71
10,000	137.76	113.66	103.22	98.02	95.24
15,000	206.63	170.49	154.83	147.02	142.85
20,000	275.51	227.32	206.44	196.03	190.47
25,000	344.38	284.15	258.05	245.03	238.09
30,000	413.26	340.98	309.66	294.04	285.70
35,000	482.13	397.81	361.27	343.04	333.32
40,000	551.01	454.64	412.88	392.05	380.93
45,000	619.88	511.47	464.49	441.06	428.55
50,000	688.76	568.30	516.10	490.06	476.17
55,000	757.63	625.13	567.71	539.07	523.78
60,000	826.51	681.96	619.32	588.07	571.40
65,000	895.38	738.79	670.93	637.08	619.02
70,000	964.26	795.62	722.54	686.08	666.63
75,000	1,033.13	852.45	774.15	735.09	714.25
80,000	1,102.01	909.28	825.76	784.10	761.86
85,000	1,170.88	966.11	877.37	833.10	809.48
90,000	1,239.76	1,022.94	928.97	882.11	857.10
95,000	1,308.63	1,079.77	980.58	931.11	904.71
100,000	1,377.51	1,136.60	1,032.19	980.12	952.33
110,000	1,515.26	1,250.26	1,135.41	1,078.13	1,047.56
120,000	1,653.01	1,363.92	1,238.63	1,176.14	1,142.79
125,000	1,721.88	1,420.75	1,290.24	1,225.15	1,190.41
130,000	1,790.76	1,477.58	1,341.85	1,274.15	1,238.03
140,000	1,928.51	1,591.24	1,445.07	1,372.16	1,333.26
150,000	2,066.26	1,704.90	1,548.29	1,470.17	1,428.49
160,000	2,204.01	1,818.56	1,651.51	1,568.19	1,523.72
170,000	2,341.76	1,932.22	1,754.73	1,666.20	1,618.95
175,000	2,410.63	1,989.05	1,806.33	1,715.20	1,666.57
180,000	2,479.51	2,045.88	1,857.94	1,764.21	1,714.19
190,000	2,617.26	2,159.54	1,961.16	1,862.22	1,809.42
200,000	2,755.01	2,273.20	2,064.38	1,960.23	1,904.65
220,000	3,030.51	2,500.52	2,270.82	2,156.25	2,095.12
225,000	3,099.38	2,557.35	2,322.43	2,205.26	2,142.73
230,000	3,168.26	2,614.18	2,374.04	2,254.27	2,190.35
240,000	3,306.01	2,727.84	2,477.26	2,352.28	2,285.58
$250,000	3,443.76	2,841.50	2,580.48	2,450.29	2,380.81

SOURCE: Modified from *McGraw-Hill's Interest Amortization Tables*, 2nd ed., by Jack C. Estes and Dennis R. Kelley (McGraw-Hill, 1993), pages 52–55 and 100–103. Reprinted by permission of McGraw-Hill, Inc.

drugs, car expenses, groceries, utilities, investments, travel, clothing, and more.

The New Century Family Money Book, by Jonathan D. Pond (Dell Publishing, 1995, $19.95). A brain-power shopper's encyclopedia. Don't get turned off by its size. Read what applies to you.

WHAT MAKES A GOOD COMPARISON SHOPPER?

As I explained earlier, without time even a born-to-shop shopper is hobbled to hurried and unwise purchases. The clock race prevents thorough comparison shopping. Yet, time alone won't turn a simple spender into a comparison shopper. A good comparison shopper has the appetite for it. She or he must have a real itch to find and buy the most and best with the least amount of money. Unless you find bargain shopping at least as much fun as a good movie, you probably won't have the pluck and urge to keep at it. Comparison shopping is *fun* to the born shopper; it's boring and abasing to the not-yet-enlightened spender.

Principles of good money management haven't changed much since Biblical times. Read Proverbs 31:10–31 for a description of what it takes to balance a household's books. Verses 14 and 16 say it best:

> She brings home food from out-of-the-way places as merchant ships do. (Translation: She brings home hard-to-find bargains like a delivery truck.)

> She looks at land and buys it, and with the money she has earned she plants a vineyard. (Translation: She watches for good buys and carefully invests the money she has saved.)
>
> —Good News Bible (TEV)

Martin, a university economics professor, and his wife, Judy, a buyer for a large department store, had fast-paced schedules that left little time for careful spending. In fact, they felt comfortable enough about their income to believe "shopping" wasn't necessary. If they needed it, they bought it and never looked back. Even so, they were dismayed (and a little ashamed) to learn they spent an extra $500 per month as a result of quick spending habits. To avoid the lines at the supermarket they had become Qwik-Stop Shop regulars. They continually overspent on antiques for their Victorian home because they didn't have time to research and attend auctions. And because they didn't want to waste time mall hopping, they regularly ordered from overpriced specialty catalogs. They also never considered just a few phone calls to check out less expensive insurance rates or references and prices when they had remodeling or repair work done to their house. Having a Ph.D. in economics and being a professional buyer didn't make Martin and Judy smart spenders.

ADD IT UP

Brad and Sally were both good comparison shoppers, but when time became scarce they lost $170 per month

BRAD AND SALLY'S MONTHLY RUSHED SHOPPING EXPENSE ($)

Automobiles, transportation	____
Bank and credit card fees	10
Clothing, jewelry, and other personal-upkeep expense	25
Entertainment, recreation, vacations	____
Furniture	____
Gasoline	____
Gifts	____
Groceries	50
Health care	____
Housing	____
Household appliances	____
Insurance (all kinds)	10
Interest rates on loans, including credit cards	80
Investments, retirement plans	____
Taxes	____
Timesavers	____
Utilities (gas, electric, telephone)	____
Other	____
Total Monthly JRE	$175

NOTE: Do not list expense if it is included in another chapter. Divide annual costs by 12 (months).

to rushed shopping. Sally lost $50 per month on rushed decisions in the grocery store and another $25 because she no longer had time to shop at garage sales for children's clothing and miscellaneous items. (Dedicated garage-salers will have higher numbers here.) They ne-

YOUR MONTHLY RUSHED SHOPPING EXPENSE

Automobiles, transportation	______
Bank and credit card fees	______
Clothing, jewelry, and other personal-upkeep expenses	______
Entertainment, recreation, vacations	______
Furniture	______
Gasoline	______
Gifts	______
Groceries	______
Health care	______
Housing	______
Household appliances	______
Insurance (all kinds)	______
Interest rates on loans, including credit cards	______
Investments, retirement plans	______
Taxes	______
Timesavers	______
Utilities (gas, electric, telephone)	______
Other	______
Total Monthly JRE	$______ *

NOTE: Do not include expense if it is listed in another chapter. Divide annual costs by 12 (months).
* ENTER this number as a negative on the rushed shopping row on Your Second-Income JREs worksheet, pages 12–13.

glected to shop for less expensive auto insurance and less expensive bank and credit card fees, which resulted in losses of $120 per year or $10 per month for each. They also got in a huge hurry to buy the dishwasher and paid $100 too much, but since that cost is included in chapter 4, Timesavers, it's not listed here. Worst of all, they never got around to refinancing their house at a lower interest rate when rates dropped, losing $80 per month.

It may be difficult to estimate figures for this chapter because savings not realized are intangible. Be as honest as possible with your own rushed shopping costs.

Your expenses may be flashing red numbers already, and there's much more bad news yet to come.

6

REWARDS

A WORLD WAR II Rosie the Riveter brought her daughter a candy bar every night. The candy bar, she said, was to compensate for having a working mother and a father away at war. Somehow, Rosie felt guilty for her family's upturned circumstances, and the five-cent candy bar was a gift to make up for the more important things lacking in their lives. The candy often went uneaten, until Rosie ate it, illustrating the futility of reward-guilt buying. Even so, she continued the practice because it was the only conscience-easing gesture she could afford, and she liked candy.

Reward-guilt buying for ourselves and others is another invisible second-income expense. In the nineties, though, the buys don't come as cheap as five-cent candy bars. Nevertheless, working parents are still likely to reward-guilt buy, some to financial downfall. We reward ourselves and spouses with unnecessary purchases because of the pressure and turmoil our second income has generated, and because we *deserve* it. We guilt buy for our children to replace the time we cannot give them, and because they *deserve* it. When's the last time you came home from a business trip empty-handed?

The rationalization goes something like this: Johnny merits a pair of $140 Air Jordans (vs. a $25 pair from Payless Shoesource), because he misses so much with both of us working; Jenny is entitled to a ski trip with all the money we're making; I, by right, should have that Gucci handbag because I work so hard; George has earned those expensive golf clubs for all the housework he helps with. . . .

Financial goals and reward-guilt buys are easily confused. A reward-guilt buy is often preceded by the word *deserve* or one of its synonyms. (Substitute the word *deserve* in each of the examples above and notice how nicely it fits.) Most important, a reward-guilt buy has no connection with financial goals. Not many of us work to buy candy bars or Air Jordans. Often, case in point the candy bars, our family would be as well or better off without them. Check your list of financial goals on page 14 so that you stay on target. You may have listed as a financial goal an item that is more accurately a reward-guilt buy. If your financial goal is to send the kids to college and you find yourself taking an ocean cruise because you've worked so hard, then the trip may be a reward-guilt buy. You can have, of course, several financial goals; both the tuition and vacations may qualify as such. But the line between goals and reward-guilt buys can be blurry; you'll need total honesty to arrive at an accurate income profile. The cruise may convince you the kids shouldn't get it all, and you may want to revise your financial goals to include nicer vacations. Remember, though, that goals you list are not necessarily ones you can afford. Chapter 13 will reveal if the spendable portion of your second income will support your goals. The vacations may cost the kids' tuition!

Even purchases that do not achieve financial goals will cross chapter lines; how you classify them is personal choice. Hence: Little Susie deserves the most expensive day care; list that expense under child care (chapter 1). You deserve a Gucci handbag; under personal upkeep (chapter 2). George deserves a riding lawn mower; list that under timesavers (chapter 4). Or the preceding examples can be listed under rewards. If the buy is justified with *deserve,* it is probably a reward-guilt buy and more correctly listed as a reward in this chapter. The overarching issue, however, is to be sure you enter the cost *somewhere* and recognize it as a job-related expense. The Gucci handbag may be an unnecessary addition to your work wardrobe, and therefore, in no way a personal-upkeep JRE. Unless you have solid evidence that little Susie will be better off attending the Royalty Day-Care Center, the cost above the Bourgeois Day-Care Center is more accurately a reward-guilt buy. If the Royalty Center is clearly better for Susie, its entire cost should be listed under child care (chapter 1).

All babies are born preprogrammed to squeeze reward-guilt buys from their parents. By the time they become teenagers they have developed sophisticated tactics that range in intensity from gentle breezes to full-scale hurricanes. Second incomes are often needed to provide a decent standard of living and education for our children. Beyond this come all degrees of reward-guilt buys instigated by children with well-intentioned parents. You may wake up to realize the extra money has all gone to turn your preschooler's bedroom into a Toys "R" Us outlet, a new addition on the house is needed for your teenage daughter's closet, and your son is spending spring break in Europe. All this can mean an empty college fund.

Reward-guilt buys can cost only a few dollars. Or they can be financial icebergs, innocent in appearance but capable of ruining our chances of attaining financial goals. One couple gives each of their kids fifty cents every Saturday to buy ice cream bars; another couple buys each kid a new car when the child turns sixteen. Neither the ice cream nor the cars are likely financial goals. If they are actually reward-guilt buys generated by the second income, they should be listed as such. Identification of reward-guilt buys will give a more reliable picture of a second income's ability to achieve genuine financial aims.

A couple in the public eye due to the wife's political career felt it necessary to send their child to a private school. The decision was based on the child's need for privacy and safety, and most assuredly, the guilt the parents would have experienced if their daughter's security were in danger. The tuition cost should be counted as a JRE if a lower economic and social position would eliminate the need for such a high-priced education. Of course, this type of expense isn't limited to the well-to-do. If everyone in your economic circle is buying the kids Nintendos or sending them to high-priced summer camps, you're more likely to feel guilty for not doing the same. This is how more money costs more money.

Reward-guilt buys can also be contagious between family members. An overstressed worker rewards himself with ongoing purchases of new CDs to unwind by during his commute home. His wife notices his growing collection and decides she has also earned the right to unwind and insists on ordering in pizza every Friday night. He sees the pizza as justification to buy a better CD player. She sees the CD player as evidence they can afford new carpet. . . . Keeping even on reward buys can turn into a cold war in which the buys might more honestly be labeled *get-even* buys. An "if you deserve that, then I deserve this" attitude can lead to money problems that threaten your marriage.

The rewards row of the Second-Income Job-Related Expenses chart (pages 10–11) shows the effects of reward-guilt buying. Best examples—those people who don't fall prey—have no expenditures. But, as with chapter 5, Rushed Shopping, Typical Case outlay tends to rise with income. The larger the income, the more we tend to reward ourselves and guilt buy for others.

ADD IT UP

Brad and Sally hired a sitter ($20) and went to see a movie ($15) and out to eat ($25) once a month more often than before Sally began working. The extra evening was an escape from their responsibilities. They *deserved* it!

Sally also spent $10 more per month on junk food for the kids (sweetened cereal, cookies, ice cream, etc.) and another $10 on miscellaneous toys and video rentals. At Christmas they spent an extra $240 on a battery-operated car for their three-year-old and a rocking horse for the baby ($240 ÷ 12 months = $20).

BRAD AND SALLY'S MONTHLY REWARD-GUILT EXPENSE ($)

Personal upkeep	
You and spouse	____
Children	____
Recreation and entertainment	35
Vacations	____
Transportation, automobiles	____
Food	
Eating out	25
At home	10
Toys	10
Gifts	20
Home furnishings	____
Other	____
Other	____
Total Monthly JRE	$100

NOTE: Do not include expenses that are financial goals or those you have listed in other chapters. Divide annual costs by 12 (months).

YOUR MONTHLY REWARD-GUILT EXPENSE ($)

Personal upkeep	
You and spouse	______
Children	______
Recreation and entertainment	______
Vacations	______
Transportation, automobiles	______
Food	
Eating out	______
At home	______
Toys	______
Gifts	______
Home furnishings	______
Other	______
Other	______
Total Monthly JRE	$______*

NOTE: Do not include expenses that are financial goals or those you have listed in other chapters. Divide annual costs by 12 (months).
* ENTER this number as a negative on the rewards row on Your Second-Income JREs worksheet, pages 12–13.

Two-income families often have gross incomes that convince them that they can afford reward-guilt buys. Working moms sometimes even feel stingy if they don't reward-guilt buy for their families.

By now, so many deductions may have eroded your income that you're starting to see the emptiness of your pay envelopes, and the peril in confusing reward-guilt buys with financial goals.

7

Federal Income Tax

Tax differences lead the way in reasons second incomes are so often overvalued, and they also account for why Uncle Sam courts second incomers. Uncle's affections are closely linked to the well-kept secret that second incomes often pay a true or effective tax rate that is two to three times higher than first incomes! This startling difference in true tax rates is concealed by mixing figures for two incomes together on one joint return. Each income's deductions and credits are combined and commingled with the other, disguising the two separate rates.

Thus, most joint filers simply assume amounts withheld from paychecks accurately indicate the tax paid by each income. Or they prorate their total tax bill according to the value of their two separate incomes to estimate their separate tax liabilities. For example: the first-income partner, earning three-fifths the total income, assumes he or she is paying three-fifths the total tax bill. Yet, in fact, the numbers are often reversed. The first income, amounting to three-fifths of the total income, may be responsible for only two-fifths of the total tax bill; the second income, amounting to two-fifths of the total income, may be responsible for three-fifths of the total tax bill! As I said earlier, tax differences head the list of reasons why second incomes are so often overrated.

Why do second incomes pay higher effective tax rates than first incomes? Because exemptions, deductions, and other adjustments can cut a first income's *taxable* amount in half, resulting in a true or effective tax rate of half the official rate. These subtractions from taxable income (unless a *direct* result of the second income, e.g., the child-care credit or second-income deductible job expense) are credited entirely to the first income because they would apply with or without the second income's presence. Because you would, for instance, claim a mortgage interest deduction whether you had one income or two, it makes sense to subtract that deduction from the first income so that the extra tax cost resulting from the second income can be identified.

Another reason for the higher effective tax rates on second incomes: The first income may use all available space within say the 15 percent bracket and thus push the second income into the 28 percent bracket. The IRS makes it sound simple enough, though: The higher your income, the higher your *official* income tax bracket—15, 28, 31, 36, or 39.6 percent. Uncle Sam will never simplify tax laws so that second incomers easily recognize their *real* tax rates as compared to first income rates because his coffers profit so much from second incomes.

Marcy and Rich (the couple in chapters 1 and 4), who earned $120,000, are prime examples of what taxes can do to a second income. Because Rich wanted to take a leave of absence from his job, he and Marcy decided to count her income as first and his income as second so that they could see the effect Rich's not earning a paycheck would have on their lifestyle. They each earned $60,000. Marcy paid only about $5,000 federal income tax because her $60,000 income—after deductions and exemptions were subtracted—remained in the 15 percent bracket. Rich paid taxes of almost $15,000 on his $60,000 income because he had fewer deductions and his income fell mostly in the 28 percent bracket. (Marcy's effective tax rate: $5,000 ÷ $60,000 = 8.3 percent; Rich's effective tax rate: $15,000 ÷ $60,000 = 25 percent.) Knowing the tax cost on Rich's income (state taxes took another $5,000 bite) was important if Marcy and Rich were to see their way clear to living on one income.

Not every couple's effective tax rates are so different, though. Julie, the part-time music teacher in chapter 4, and her husband, Greg, got a slightly better ratio than Rich and Marcy. Both Julie's and Greg's incomes stayed in the 15 percent bracket. Still, Greg's income benefited more from exemptions and deductions, which cut his taxable income to less than half his gross income. So Julie paid an effective rate of 13 percent, while Greg paid 7 percent.

Federal tax laws are so complicated that most taxpayers see and remember only the last line (refund or amount owed) on their tax returns. The IRS allows a deduction, then multiplies it by a strange percentage, refers to another form, subtracts numbers which seem to drop from the sky, and transfers numbers to still other pages; the numbers go up and down, around and around. The process is no accident; the more confused you become, the more likely you are to not recognize how much and at what rate you've paid.

Yet Uncle Sam feigns concern for second incomers by throwing scraps of encouragement through credits and deductions—most notably, the child-care credit, or deduction, or both. Often, however, job deductions are no more than elaborate mirages. Uncle Sam's stakes are too high to let second incomers discover that they are the juiciest bones in his larder.

This book is not a dreary guide to tax planning and preparation. Chapters 7 and 8 are meant solely to give a quick and easy method of *estimating* what your second income costs in federal and state taxes. Take heart and realize that in this book, the number juggling will never get worse than what's in these chapters. The numbers are important and worth mastering, for they may be your largest job-related expenses.

To understand and apply explanations in this book to your own situation, have a copy of your last year's federal and state tax returns (with accompanying tax rate schedules and tables) nearby as you read. If the thought of understanding very basic tax principles gives you heart palpitations, you should get professional help later

cathy® by Cathy Guisewite

(with the taxes), but for now, remain calm and give it your best try.

SOME *VERY* BASIC TAX INFO

Before you can estimate tax cost on a second income, you'll have to cope with a little tax gibberish. *Estimate* is a key word because few of us are interested in reading all

> To take total control of your tax life you'll need to read much more than this book can provide. The IRS's "Your Federal Income Tax," Publication No. 17 (free by calling 1-800-TAX-FORM) is a good place to begin. For easier reading and more loophole directions, you'll need to read a tax manual written by someone other than the IRS. The *Ernst & Young Tax Guide, J. K. Lasser's Your Income Tax,* and the *H&R Block Income Tax Guide* are all good references, updated annually, and available in bookstores during tax season. Their prices are in the $15 to $16 range.

the ins and outs that would produce an accurate number for absolutely everyone. Reading too much detail about others' extenuating tax problems would have us all sticking pencils up our noses. Because most ins and outs apply to a limited number of filers, chances are the following steps will give you a fairly accurate result. If you find yourself filling out a special form or line, or tax laws have changed since the printing of this book (not unlikely since budget battles are being waged as the book goes to press), you may have to adjust your final numbers to reflect these complications—or, better yet, consult a tax professional.

Joint vs. Separate Returns

Almost invariably, married, two-income couples find filing a joint income tax return to be simpler, and usually more economical, than filing two separate returns. Filing separate returns would seem to provide straight numbers on a second income's tax cost, but a host of restrictions apply to spouses living together and filing separate returns (most notably, the child-care credit is not allowed). Second incomers filing separately also must claim their own personal exemption ($2,650 in 1997), which further confuses how much tax the first income would have paid alone. As a result, separate returns are not an accurate means of finding a second income's true tax cost.

Which Form?

Married taxpayers have a choice of using either the "easy" Form 1040EZ, the "short" Form 1040A, or the "long" Form 1040. You should use the long 1040 Form if your taxable income is $50,000 or more, if itemized deductions exceed the standard deduction, or if you have income or credits that cannot be entered on the short 1040A Form. Only couples with no dependents can use Form 1040EZ. Check form instructions if in doubt. Aggressive taxpayers will almost always use Form 1040, and examples in this book will use Form 1040—but where applicable, corresponding line numbers for Form 1040A will be listed.

Tax Tables vs. Schedule Y–1

When filing official tax returns, most taxpayers with taxable income of less than $100,000 *must* use the tax tables in the instruction books to figure tax owed. That's a *nice* rule, because the tax tables take the computation out of figuring what you owe. While reading this book, however, all income levels will gain a clearer view of the pillage by referring to Schedule Y–1, which involves some figuring, in the Form 1040 instruction book. Schedule Y–1, no matter what your income, will give a sharper

1997 SCHEDULE Y–1

Schedule Y-1—Use if your filing status is **Married filing jointly** or **Qualifying widow(er)**

If the amount on Form 1040, line 38, is: *Over—*	*But not over—*	Enter on Form 1040, line 39	*of the amount over—*
$0	$41,200	.... **15%**	**$0**
41,200	99,600	**$6,180.00 + 28%**	**41,200**
99,600	151,750	**22,532.00 + 31%**	**99,600**
151,750	271,050	**38,698.50 + 36%**	**151,750**
271,050	....	**81,646.50 + 39.6%**	**271,050**

view of your position within bracket lines than the tax tables.

If you've thrown away last year's supporting tax tables, go ahead and use Schedule Y–1, because numbers arrived at here are not for official use. Because the tax tables are given in $50 steps, results using Schedule Y–1 may vary from tax table numbers by as much as $8. Don't let these small differences in tax owed—using the two different methods—cause you to misplace your pencil.

BRAD, SALLY, AND UNCLE SAM'S MIRRORS

Brad and Sally knew the cutoff point between the 15 percent and 28 percent brackets was $41,200 (see Schedule Y–1). Because Brad's income was $30,000 the previous year, they mistakenly believed a large part of Sally's $20,000 income would be taxed at the 28 percent rate. But their itemized deductions and exemptions reduced Brad's *taxable* income to $10,000, making it possible for Sally to earn $31,200 ($41,200 – $10,000 = $31,200) before any of Sally's income reached the 28 percent bracket.

Even though both their incomes fell within the *official* 15 percent bracket, Sally's income was taxed at a higher *true* rate because deductions and exemptions cut Brad's *taxable* income to less than half of his original income. Their true tax rate difference would have been even larger if Brad's income had been high enough to push Sally's income into the 28 percent bracket, or if Sally had no child-care credit or retirement deduction. As Brad's income and IRS tax rates change through the years,

Sally's income will reflect a different (and probably higher) tax rate. So, you should refigure your federal income tax JRE annually if you're serious about knowing where your money goes.

Uncle Sam appeases taxpayers with mirrored illusions of tax deductions and credits, leaving more gullible taxpayers persuaded that their tax credits and deductions are reducing qualifying expenses, while, at the same time, lowering their taxes. Brad and Sally received a tax credit for 20 percent on most of their child-care expense, which they mentally subtracted from their child-care costs each month, and then again from their taxes when they filed their tax return. Although the credit was real, it was not twice a savings. Indeed, deductions often never make it through the sieve of math exercises to be counted at all. The value of the $900 deduction for work-related expenses that Brad and Sally shared was reduced to *nothing* by a fancy math trick. Still, Brad and Sally continued to trust that their work-related expenses weren't really costing anything, and in separate thoughts and on different days they fancied that their tax bill was reduced by the same deduction.

THE EASIEST WAY

The quickest way to find a second income's tax cost on a joint return:

1. Hold your nose.
2. Refigure your joint tax return by removing all entries originating from second income.

3. Subtract the tax paid by first income from the total tax paid by combined incomes (the difference between numbers on line 53, Form 1040; or line 28, Form 1040A; or line 10, Form 1040EZ). The difference is your second income's tax cost.

This said, the IRS is hoping you are now thinking how nicely these pages will fit in the bottom of a bird cage. After lining the bird cage, you may proceed through a maze of calculations in search of an easier way. If your bird is constipated this may not be a fatal mistake.

Uncle Sam counts on you sticking your pencil about now. (Note precautionary step 1 above.) Hold your pencil, formidable as the above directions sound. Because numbers are readily available on combined incomes (if you've found last year's tax return), subtracting the second income and its effects, and refiguring tax on only the first income is a fifteen-minute job for taxpayers with no unusual entries.

Consult a tax professional, however, if you have any doubts at all about the accuracy of your figures, or if your tax return is complicated. Space limitations and the author's uncredentialed interest in taxes limit covering every circumstance. (A good time to get expert help is while you're having your taxes done. With a computer tax program, your tax preparer can probably remove all entries originating from second income from your joint return [step 2, page 94] in a matter of minutes. She or he may not even charge for this small extra service.)

ADD IT UP

Brad and Sally's Form 1040 (see pages 97–98) shows how they redid their return, removing all entries originating from Sally's income (step 2, page 94). Use pages 99–100 for your own numbers. If you've thrown away last year's tax tables, use Schedule Y–1, page 92, for figuring tax owed.

Single-Income Couples: Single-income couples may find approximate tax cost on a potential second income by *adding* projected second income and its effects to their tax return. First, however, it may be necessary to read this chapter's postscript #2, Child-Care Tax Benefits, pages 107–117, to understand and figure the value of a future child-care credit or deduction. As in the above steps, the total tax difference between the two sets of numbers is the second income's estimated tax cost.

BRAD AND SALLY'S 1040 TAX RETURN

Form 1040 (M) Department of the Treasury—Internal Revenue Service
U.S. Individual Income Tax Return **1997** (99) IRS Use Only—Do not write or staple in this space.

For the year Jan. 1–Dec. 31, 1997, or other tax year beginning , 1997, ending , 19 OMB No. 1545-0074

Label (See instructions on page 10.) **Use the IRS label.** Otherwise, please print or type.

LABEL HERE		
Your first name and initial: Bradley R.	Last name: Smith	Your social security number: 123 00 4567
If a joint return, spouse's first name and initial: Sally B.	Last name: Smith	Spouse's social security number: 234 00 5678
Home address (number and street). If you have a P.O. box, see page 10.: 429 Mill Rd.	Apt. no.	
City, town or post office, state, and ZIP code. If you have a foreign address, see page 10.: Hometown, N.Y. 01040		

For help in finding line instructions, see pages 2 and 3 in the booklet.

Presidential Election Campaign (See page 10.)

	Yes	No
Do you want $3 to go to this fund?		✓
If a joint return, does your spouse want $3 to go to this fund?		✓

Note: *Checking "Yes" will not change your tax or reduce your refund.*

Filing Status* — Check only one box.

- ① 1 [ ] Single
- ② 2 [✓] Married filing joint return (even if only one had income)
- ③ 3 [ ] Married filing separate return. Enter spouse's social security no. above and full name here. ▶
- ④ 4 [ ] Head of household (with qualifying person). (See page 10.) If the qualifying person is a child but not your dependent, enter this child's name here. ▶
- ⑤ 5 [ ] Qualifying widow(er) with dependent child (year spouse died ▶ 19). (See page 10.)

Exemptions

(6a) 6a [✓] **Yourself.** If your parent (or someone else) can claim you as a dependent on his or her tax return, **do not** check box 6a. — No. of boxes checked on 6a and 6b: 2

(6b) b [✓] **Spouse**

(6c) c **Dependents:**

(1) First name Last name	(2) Dependent's social security number	(3) Dependent's relationship to you	(4) No. of months lived in your home in 1997
Erik P. Smith	345 00 6789	Son	12
Lisa M. Smith	456 00 7890	Daughter	12

If more than six dependents, see page 10.

No. of your children on 6c who: • lived with you: 2 • did not live with you due to divorce or separation (see page 11): Dependents on 6c not entered above: Add numbers entered on lines above ▶ 4

(6d) d Total number of exemptions claimed

Income

Attach Copy B of your Forms W-2, W-2G, and 1099-R here. If you did not get a W-2, see page 12. Enclose but do not attach any payment. Also, please use Form 1040-V.

Line	Description		Amount	Sally†
(7) 7	Wages, salaries, tips, etc. Attach Form(s) W-2**	7	49,200	30,000
(8a) 8a	**Taxable** interest. Attach Schedule B if required	8a	25	25
(8b) b	**Tax-exempt** interest. DO NOT include on line 8a . . . 8b			
(9) 9	Dividends. Attach Schedule B if required	9		
10	Taxable refunds, credits, or offsets of state and local income taxes (see page 12)	10		
11	Alimony received	11		
12	Business income or (loss). Attach Schedule C or C-EZ	12		
13	Capital gain or (loss). Attach Schedule D	13		
14	Other gains or (losses). Attach Form 4797	14		
(10a) 15a	Total IRA distributions . 15a (10b) b Taxable amount (see page 13)	15b		
(11a) 16a	Total pensions and annuities 16a (11b) b Taxable amount (see page 13)	16b		
17	Rental real estate, royalties, partnerships, S corporations, trusts, etc. Attach Schedule E	17		
18	Farm income or (loss). Attach Schedule F	18		
(12) 19	Unemployment compensation	19		
(13a) 20a	Social security benefits . 20a (13b) b Taxable amount (see page 14)	20b		
21	Other income. List type and amount—see page 15	21		
(14) 22	Add the amounts in the far right column for lines 7 through 21. This is your **total income** ▶	22	49,225	30,025

Adjusted Gross Income

If line 32 is under $29,290 (under $9,770 if a child did not live with you), see EIC inst. on page 21.

(15) 23	IRA deduction (see page 16)	23			
24	Medical savings account deduction. Attach Form 8853	24			
25	Moving expenses. Attach Form 3903 or 3903-F	25			
26	One-half of self-employment tax. Attach Schedule SE	26			
27	Self-employed health insurance deduction (see page 17)	27			
28	Keogh and self-employed SEP and SIMPLE plans	28			
29	Penalty on early withdrawal of savings	29			
30a	Alimony paid b Recipient's SSN ▶	30a			
31	Add lines 23 through 30a			31	
(16) 32	Subtract line 31 from line 22. This is your **adjusted gross income** ▶			32	49,225 / 30,025

For Privacy Act and Paperwork Reduction Act Notice, see page 38. Cat. No. 11320B Form **1040** (1997)

* Circled numbers identify corresponding line numbers on the short 1040A Form.

** Brad and Sally's total wages ($30,000 + $20,000) were reduced by $800 (Sally's retirement plan contribution).

† Numbers in shaded boxes show Sally's income and its effects subtracted to reveal tax on Brad's income alone (line 53).

BRAD AND SALLY'S 1040 TAX RETURN (page 2)

Form 1040 (1997) — Page 2

Tax Computation

Line	Description	Amount	Revised
(17) 33	Amount from line 32 (adjusted gross income)	49,225	30,025
(18a) 34a	Check if: ☐ You were 65 or older, ☐ Blind; ☐ Spouse was 65 or older, ☐ Blind. Add the number of boxes checked above and enter the total here ▶ 34a		
(18b) b	If you are married filing separately and your spouse itemizes deductions or you were a dual-status alien, see page 18 and check here ▶ 34b ☐		
(19) 35	Enter the larger of your: **Itemized deductions** from Schedule A, line 28, **OR** **Standard deduction** shown below for your filing status. **But** see page 18 if you checked any box on line 34a or 34b **or** someone can claim you as a dependent. • Single—$4,150 • Married filing jointly or Qualifying widow(er)—$6,900 • Head of household—$6,050 • Married filing separately—$3,450	9,425	9,425*
(20) 36	Subtract line 35 from line 33	39,800	20,600
(21) 37	If line 33 is $90,900 or less, multiply $2,650 by the total number of exemptions claimed on line 6d. If line 33 is over $90,900, see the worksheet on page 19 for the amount to enter	10,600	10,600
(22) 38	**Taxable income.** Subtract line 37 from line 36. If line 37 is more than line 36, enter -0-	29,200	10,000
(23) 39	**Tax.** See page 19. Check if any tax from a ☐ Form(s) 8814 b ☐ Form 4972 ▶	4,384	1,504

If you want the IRS to figure your tax, see page 18.

Credits

Line	Description	Amount	Revised
(24a) 40	Credit for child and dependent care expenses. Attach Form 2441	960**	-0-
(24b) 41	Credit for the elderly or the disabled. Attach Schedule R		
(24c) 42	Adoption credit. Attach Form 8839		
43	Foreign tax credit. Attach Form 1116		
44	Other. Check if from a ☐ Form 3800 b ☐ Form 8396 c ☐ Form 8801 d ☐ Form (specify) ______		
(24d) 45	Add lines 40 through 44	960	-0-
(25) 46	Subtract line 45 from line 39. If line 45 is more than line 39, enter -0- ▶	3,424	1,504

Other Taxes

Line	Description	Amount	Revised
47	Self-employment tax. Attach Schedule SE		†
48	Alternative minimum tax. Attach Form 6251		
49	Social security and Medicare tax on tip income not reported to employer. Attach Form 4137		
50	Tax on qualified retirement plans (including IRAs) and MSAs. Attach Form 5329 if required		
(26) 51	Advance earned income credit payments from Form(s) W-2		
(27) 52	Household employment taxes. Attach Schedule H		
(28) 53	Add lines 46 through 52. This is your **total tax** ▶	3,424	1,504

The important numbers! (line 53)

Payments

Attach Forms W-2, W-2G, and 1099-R on the front.

Line	Description	Amount	Revised
(29a) 54	Federal income tax withheld from Forms W-2 and 1099	4,062	2,001‡
(29b) 55	1997 estimated tax payments and amount applied from 1996 return		
(29c) 56a	**Earned income credit.** Attach Schedule EIC if you have a qualifying child (29d) b Nontaxable earned income: amount ▶ ______ and type ▶ ______		§
57	Amount paid with Form 4868 (request for extension)		
58	Excess social security and RRTA tax withheld (see page 27)		
59	Other payments. Check if from a ☐ Form 2439 b ☐ Form 4136		
(29e) 60	Add lines 54, 55, 56a, 57, 58, and 59. These are your **total payments** ▶	4,062	2,001‡

Refund

Have it directly deposited! See page 27 and fill in 62b, 62c, and 62d.

Line	Description	Amount	Revised
(30) 61	If line 60 is more than line 53, subtract line 53 from line 60. This is the amount you **OVERPAID**	638	497‡
(31a) 62a	Amount of line 61 you want **REFUNDED TO YOU** ▶	638	497‡
(31b) b	Routing number ______ (31c) c Type: ☐ Checking ☐ Savings		
(31d) d	Account number ______		
(32) 63	Amount of line 61 you want **APPLIED TO YOUR 1998 ESTIMATED TAX** ▶		

Amount You Owe

Line	Description	Amount	Revised
(33) 64	If line 53 is more than line 60, subtract line 60 from line 53. This is the **AMOUNT YOU OWE.** For details on how to pay, see page 27 ▶		‡
(34) 65	Estimated tax penalty. Also include on line 64		

Sign Here

Under penalties of perjury, I declare that I have examined this return and accompanying schedules and statements, and to the best of my knowledge and belief, they are true, correct, and complete. Declaration of preparer (other than taxpayer) is based on all information of which preparer has any knowledge.

Keep a copy of this return for your records.

Your signature	Date	Your occupation
Bradley R. Smith	2/20/98	Advertising Sales
Spouse's signature. If a joint return, BOTH must sign.	**Date**	**Spouse's occupation**
Sally B. Smith	2/20/98	Social Worker

Paid Preparer's Use Only

Preparer's signature	Date	Check if self-employed ☐	Preparer's social security no.
Firm's name (or yours if self-employed) and address			EIN
			ZIP code

* Don't refigure itemized deductions unless you see the need after reading this chapter's postscript #1, pages 103–106.

** How to figure this credit is explained in postscript #2, pages 107–117.

† If either income is from self-employment, numbers can get skewed here because the self-employment (Social Security) tax is included in total tax, line 53. It may be best to get help from a tax professional to sort this out. (See note, page 102.)

‡ Ignore. Amounts withheld, owed, or to be refunded have nothing to do with how much your tax was, except that their differences *sometimes* reveal tax paid.

§ Ignore for now. See postscript #1, pages 103–106, and chapter 12.

YOUR 1040 TAX RETURN
(Or insert your 1040A or 1040EZ tax return)

Form **1040** Department of the Treasury—Internal Revenue Service
U.S. Individual Income Tax Return **1997** (99) IRS Use Only—Do not write or staple in this space.

For the year Jan. 1–Dec. 31, 1997, or other tax year beginning , 1997, ending , 19 OMB No. 1545-0074

Label (See instructions on page 10.) **Use the IRS label.** Otherwise, please print or type.

LABEL HERE

Your first name and initial	Last name	Your social security number
If a joint return, spouse's first name and initial	Last name	Spouse's social security number
Home address (number and street). If you have a P.O. box, see page 10.	Apt. no.	**For help in finding line instructions, see pages 2 and 3 in the booklet.**
City, town or post office, state, and ZIP code. If you have a foreign address, see page 10.		

Presidential Election Campaign (See page 10.)

	Yes	No	*Note: Checking "Yes" will not change your tax or reduce your refund.*
Do you want $3 to go to this fund?			
If a joint return, does your spouse want $3 to go to this fund?			

Filing Status

Check only one box.

1 ☐ Single
2 ☐ Married filing joint return (even if only one had income)
3 ☐ Married filing separate return. Enter spouse's social security no. above and full name here. ▶
4 ☐ Head of household (with qualifying person). (See page 10.) If the qualifying person is a child but not your dependent, enter this child's name here. ▶
5 ☐ Qualifying widow(er) with dependent child (year spouse died ▶ 19). (See page 10.)

Exemptions

6a ☐ **Yourself.** If your parent (or someone else) can claim you as a dependent on his or her tax return, **do not** check box 6a
b ☐ **Spouse**

No. of boxes checked on 6a and 6b ____

c **Dependents:**

(1) First name Last name	(2) Dependent's social security number	(3) Dependent's relationship to you	(4) No. of months lived in your home in 1997

If more than six dependents, see page 10.

No. of your children on 6c who:
- lived with you ____
- did not live with you due to divorce or separation (see page 11) ____

Dependents on 6c not entered above ____

Add numbers entered on lines above ▶ ☐

d Total number of exemptions claimed

Income

Attach Copy B of your Forms W-2, W-2G, and 1099-R here.

If you did not get a W-2, see page 12.

Enclose but do not attach any payment. Also, please use Form 1040-V.

7	Wages, salaries, tips, etc. Attach Form(s) W-2		7	
8a	**Taxable** interest. Attach Schedule B if required		8a	
b	**Tax-exempt** interest. DO NOT include on line 8a	8b		
9	Dividends. Attach Schedule B if required		9	
10	Taxable refunds, credits, or offsets of state and local income taxes (see page 12)		10	
11	Alimony received		11	
12	Business income or (loss). Attach Schedule C or C-EZ		12	
13	Capital gain or (loss). Attach Schedule D		13	
14	Other gains or (losses). Attach Form 4797		14	
15a	Total IRA distributions 15a	b Taxable amount (see page 13)	15b	
16a	Total pensions and annuities 16a	b Taxable amount (see page 13)	16b	
17	Rental real estate, royalties, partnerships, S corporations, trusts, etc. Attach Schedule E		17	
18	Farm income or (loss). Attach Schedule F		18	
19	Unemployment compensation		19	
20a	Social security benefits 20a	b Taxable amount (see page 14)	20b	
21	Other income. List type and amount—see page 15		21	
22	Add the amounts in the far right column for lines 7 through 21. This is your **total income** ▶		22	

Adjusted Gross Income

If line 32 is under $29,290 (under $9,770 if a child did not live with you), see EIC inst. on page 21.

23	IRA deduction (see page 16)	23			
24	Medical savings account deduction. Attach Form 8853	24			
25	Moving expenses. Attach Form 3903 or 3903-F	25			
26	One-half of self-employment tax. Attach Schedule SE	26			
27	Self-employed health insurance deduction (see page 17)	27			
28	Keogh and self-employed SEP and SIMPLE plans	28			
29	Penalty on early withdrawal of savings	29			
30a	Alimony paid b Recipient's SSN ▶	30a			
31	Add lines 23 through 30a			31	
32	Subtract line 31 from line 22. This is your **adjusted gross income** ▶			32	

For Privacy Act and Paperwork Reduction Act Notice, see page 38. Cat. No. 11320B Form **1040** (1997)

YOUR 1040 TAX RETURN (page 2)
(Or insert your 1040A tax return, page 2)

Form 1040 (1997) Page **2**

Tax Computation

33 Amount from line 32 (adjusted gross income) . . . 33

34a Check if: ☐ **You** were 65 or older, ☐ Blind; ☐ **Spouse** was 65 or older, ☐ Blind.
Add the number of boxes checked above and enter the total here . . . ▶ **34a**

b If you are married filing separately and your spouse itemizes deductions or you were a dual-status alien, see page 18 and check here . . . ▶ **34b** ☐

35 Enter the **larger** of your: **Itemized deductions** from Schedule A, line 28, **OR** **Standard deduction** shown below for your filing status. **But** see page 18 if you checked any box on line 34a or 34b **or** someone can claim you as a dependent.
• Single—$4,150 • Married filing jointly or Qualifying widow(er)—$6,900
• Head of household—$6,050 • Married filing separately—$3,450 — 35 *

If you want the IRS to figure your tax, see page 18.

36 Subtract line 35 from line 33 . . . 36

37 If line 33 is $90,900 or less, multiply $2,650 by the total number of exemptions claimed on line 6d. If line 33 is over $90,900, see the worksheet on page 19 for the amount to enter . 37

38 **Taxable income.** Subtract line 37 from line 36. If line 37 is more than line 36, enter -0- 38

39 **Tax.** See page 19. Check if any tax from **a** ☐ Form(s) 8814 **b** ☐ Form 4972 . . ▶ 39

Credits

40 Credit for child and dependent care expenses. Attach Form 2441 — 40 **

41 Credit for the elderly or the disabled. Attach Schedule R . . 41

42 Adoption credit. Attach Form 8839 . . 42

43 Foreign tax credit. Attach Form 1116 . . 43

44 Other. Check if from **a** ☐ Form 3800 **b** ☐ Form 8396 **c** ☐ Form 8801 **d** ☐ Form (specify)________ 44

45 Add lines 40 through 44 . . . 45

46 Subtract line 45 from line 39. If line 45 is more than line 39, enter -0- . . . ▶ 46

Other Taxes

47 Self-employment tax. Attach Schedule SE . . . 47 †

48 Alternative minimum tax. Attach Form 6251 . . . 48

49 Social security and Medicare tax on tip income not reported to employer. Attach Form 4137 . 49

50 Tax on qualified retirement plans (including IRAs) and MSAs. Attach Form 5329 if required 50

51 Advance earned income credit payments from Form(s) W-2 . . . 51

52 Household employment taxes. Attach Schedule H . . . 52

53 Add lines 46 through 52. This is your **total tax** . . . ▶ 53

The important numbers!

Payments

54 Federal income tax withheld from Forms W-2 and 1099 . . 54 ‡

55 1997 estimated tax payments and amount applied from 1996 return . 55

56a **Earned income credit.** Attach Schedule EIC if you have a qualifying child **b** Nontaxable earned income: amount ▶ ________ and type ▶ ________ 56a §

Attach Forms W-2, W-2G, and 1099-R on the front.

57 Amount paid with Form 4868 (request for extension) . . . 57

58 Excess social security and RRTA tax withheld (see page 27) 58

59 Other payments. Check if from **a** ☐ Form 2439 **b** ☐ Form 4136 59

60 Add lines 54, 55, 56a, 57, 58, and 59. These are your **total payments** . . . ▶ 60 ‡

Refund

61 If line 60 is more than line 53, subtract line 53 from line 60. This is the amount you **OVERPAID** 61 ‡

62a Amount of line 61 you want **REFUNDED TO YOU** . . . ▶ 62a ‡

Have it directly deposited! See page 27 and fill in 62b, 62c, and 62d.

▶ **b** Routing number ☐☐☐☐☐☐☐☐☐ ▶ **c** Type: ☐ Checking ☐ Savings

▶ **d** Account number ☐☐☐☐☐☐☐☐☐☐☐☐☐☐☐☐☐

63 Amount of line 61 you want **APPLIED TO YOUR 1998 ESTIMATED TAX** ▶ 63

Amount You Owe

64 If line 53 is more than line 60, subtract line 60 from line 53. This is the **AMOUNT YOU OWE.** For details on how to pay, see page 27 . . . ▶ 64 ‡

65 Estimated tax penalty. Also include on line 64 . . . 65

Sign Here

Keep a copy of this return for your records.

Under penalties of perjury, I declare that I have examined this return and accompanying schedules and statements, and to the best of my knowledge and belief, they are true, correct, and complete. Declaration of preparer (other than taxpayer) is based on all information of which preparer has any knowledge.

Your signature | Date | Your occupation

Spouse's signature. If a joint return, BOTH must sign. | Date | Spouse's occupation

Paid Preparer's Use Only

Preparer's signature ▶ | Date | Check if self-employed ☐ | Preparer's social security no.

Firm's name (or yours if self-employed) and address ▶ | EIN | ZIP code

* Don't refigure itemized deductions unless you see the need after reading this chapter's postscript #1, pages 103–106.

** How to figure this credit is explained in postscript #2, pages 107–117.

† If either income is from self-employment, numbers can get skewed here because the self-employment (Social Security) tax is included in total tax, line 53. It may be best to get help from a tax professional to sort this out. (See note, page 102.)

‡ Ignore. Amounts withheld, owed, or to be refunded have nothing to do with how much your tax was, except that their differences *sometimes* reveal tax paid.

§ Ignore for now. See postscript #1, pages 103–106, and chapter 12.

Congratulations! By doing pages 99–100, you've just outsmarted Uncle Sam! Now you're ready for step 3, calculating your second income's true tax cost:

Subtract tax paid by first income from tax paid by combined incomes (the difference between numbers on line 53, Form 1040; or line 28, Form 1040A; or line 10, Form 1040EZ). *Then divide by 12 for monthly cost.*

BRAD AND SALLY'S FIGURES

$3,424	–	$1,504	=	$1,920	÷ 12 =	$160
Tax on combined incomes		Tax on first income		Tax on second income		Monthly JRE on second income

Notice that Sally earned only 40 percent of their total income, but her income was responsible for 56 percent ($1,920 ÷ $3,424) of their combined tax bill! Alarming as these numbers are, Sally's share of the tax load would have been even higher without the child-care credit and retirement deduction. The new child tax credit, worth $400 per child in 1998 and $500 per child in 1999, will further widen the differences in effective rates spouses pay. Subtracting $800 from Brad's tax liability would

YOUR FIGURES

_____	–	_____	=	_____	÷ 12 =	$ _____★
Tax on combined incomes		Tax on first income		Tax on second income		Monthly JRE on second income

★ ENTER this number as a negative on the federal taxes row on Your Second-Income JREs worksheet, pages 12–13.

leave Sally paying 73 percent ($1,920/$2,624) of their tax bill!

NOTE: Couples with self-employment income have an extra row to hoe in order to compare income tax rates and find tax owed by second income because the self-employment tax is included in total tax, line 53. Unless you're very good with numbers, get professional help with this.

If you want to hoe this row yourself:

To Compare Income Tax Rates remove self-employment tax effects (lines 26 and 47) from total tax (line 53) for both incomes. The difference between line 53 totals can then be used to determine separate income tax rates.

To Find (Income and Self-Employment) Tax Paid by Second Income, remove self-employment tax effects (lines 26 and 47) from total tax (line 53) for *only* the first income. The difference between line 53 totals will then show second income's income *and* self-employment tax. (For self-employed workers, the self-employment—Social Security—tax is included with income tax, rather than in chapter 9.)

Uncle Sam's share of second incomes is a national secret, and a large reason why it is so difficult to get ahead on a second income. If your head is throbbing right now, chances are you haven't taken time to dig through the box in the attic to find last year's tax return. *Do It Now!* Then reread this chapter, plugging in your own numbers, and see how easy this all becomes. Painful, but easy.

CHAPTER 7

POSTSCRIPT #1

THE ALTERNATIVE MINIMUM TAX
THE EARNED INCOME CREDIT
ITEMIZED DEDUCTIONS

Not everyone needs to read this postscript. Perfectionists and CPAs will probably complain though, because not every in and out is addressed in this book. Thank goodness this is true; otherwise I would have left this planet writing these pages, and you would probably join me trying to read them. Capital gains, IRA distributions and deductions, moving expenses, recapture taxes, foreign tax credits, household employment taxes, and a multitude of other issues haven't been addressed. If you need to know more, consult a tax professional.

For most of us, the foregoing information will produce an adequate estimate of tax cost on a second income. For those readers determined to be accurate to the last cent or who have mitigating circumstances, just a *little* more information is provided:

1. Line 48, Form 1040. The *Alternative Minimum Tax* may waylay couples with unusually high subtractions from taxable income. Form 6251, Alternative Minimum Tax, is the mother of all tax forms. Professional help is suggested.

2. Line 56a, Form 1040; or line 29c, Form 1040A; or line 8a, Form 1040EZ. The *Earned Income Credit* is a credit for low-income workers with earned income

below specified levels, which depend upon number of qualifying children. In 1997, workers with more than one qualifying child could earn up to $29,290 and still qualify for the EIC. When a second income pushes earned income above the designated level for your circumstance, the credit, worth as much as $3,656 in 1997, is lost. (See chapter 12 for more details on the EIC.)

3. Line 35, Form 1040. *Itemized Deductions.* Some deductions on Form 1040, Schedule A, are limited by a percentage of Adjusted Gross Income, line 33. Medical expense is reduced by 7.5 percent of AGI, casualty or theft loss by 10 percent, and job expense and most miscellaneous deductions by 2 percent. Therefore, when income is increased by a second income, these deductions are reduced. For most taxpayers these changes are insignificant. Brad and Sally lost a $768 medical expense deduction because of Sally's income (see page 105, line 4), but the loss was offset by an increase in the state income tax deduction (line 5) due to her earnings. The total difference of only $162 for itemized deductions wasn't worth the bookwork of redoing Schedule A.

Itemized deductions are limited even further on Schedule A for couples with AGIs above a specified level ($121,200 for 1997). So the increase in AGI caused by a second income takes a double whammy at itemized deductions for these couples. Redo Schedule A if you suspect there may be major changes in itemized deductions due to second income, or if you want to figure to the last cent. Then use revised itemized deductions on Form 1040, line 35, page 100. Brad and Sally's Schedule A follows on page 105, and for your numbers, a blank Schedule A, on page 106.

BRAD AND SALLY'S SCHEDULE A ITEMIZED DEDUCTIONS

SCHEDULES A&B (Form 1040) Department of the Treasury Internal Revenue Service (L)

Schedule A—Itemized Deductions

(Schedule B is on back)

▶ Attach to Form 1040. ▶ See Instructions for Schedules A and B (Form 1040).

OMB No. 1545-0074 **1997** Attachment Sequence No. **07**

Name(s) shown on Form 1040: Bradley R. & Sally B. Smith — Your social security number: 123 00 4567

Section	Line	Description	Box	Amount	Shaded	Box	Amount	Shaded
Medical and Dental Expenses		Caution: *Do not include expenses reimbursed or paid by others.*						
	1	Medical and dental expenses (see page A-1)	1	3,020	3,020 *			
	2	Enter amount from Form 1040, line 33. 2 49,225 [30,025]						
	3	Multiply line 2 above by 7.5% (.075)	3	3,692	2,252			
	4	Subtract line 3 from line 1. If line 3 is more than line 1, enter -0-				4	-0-	768
Taxes You Paid (See page A-2.)	5	State and local income taxes	5	2,025	1,095			
	6	Real estate taxes (see page A-2)	6	1,100	1,100			
	7	Personal property taxes	7	100	100			
	8	Other taxes. List type and amount ▶	8					
	9	Add lines 5 through 8				9	3,225	2,295
Interest You Paid (See page A-2.)	10	Home mortgage interest and points reported to you on Form 1098	10	5,750	5,750			
	11	Home mortgage interest not reported to you on Form 1098. If paid to the person from whom you bought the home, see page A-3 and show that person's name, identifying no., and address ▶	11					
Note: Personal interest is not deductible.	12	Points not reported to you on Form 1098. See page A-3 for special rules	12					
	13	Investment interest. Attach Form 4952 if required. (See page A-3.)	13					
	14	Add lines 10 through 13				14	5,750	5,750
Gifts to Charity If you made a gift and got a benefit for it, see page A-3.	15	Gifts by cash or check. If you made any gift of $250 or more, see page A-3	15	450	450			
	16	Other than by cash or check. If any gift of $250 or more, see page A-3. You **MUST** attach Form 8283 if over $500	16					
	17	Carryover from prior year	17					
	18	Add lines 15 through 17				18	450	450
Casualty and Theft Losses	19	Casualty or theft loss(es). Attach Form 4684. (See page A-4.)				19		
Job Expenses and Most Other Miscellaneous Deductions	20	Unreimbursed employee expenses—job travel, union dues, job education, etc. You **MUST** attach Form 2106 or 2106-EZ if required. (See page A-4.) ▶	20	900	300 **			
	21	Tax preparation fees	21					
(See page A-5 for expenses to deduct here.)	22	Other expenses—investment, safe deposit box, etc. List type and amount ▶	22					
	23	Add lines 20 through 22	23	900	300			
	24	Enter amount from Form 1040, line 33. 24 49,225 [30,025]						
	25	Multiply line 24 above by 2% (.02)	25	985	601			
	26	Subtract line 25 from line 23. If line 25 is more than line 23, enter -0-				26	-0-	-0-
Other Miscellaneous Deductions	27	Other—from list on page A-5. List type and amount ▶				27		
Total Itemized Deductions	28	Is Form 1040, line 33, over $121,200 (over $60,600 if married filing separately)? **NO.** Your deduction is not limited. Add the amounts in the far right column for lines 4 through 27. Also, enter on Form 1040, line 35, the **larger** of this amount or your standard deduction. **YES.** Your deduction may be limited. See page A-5 for the amount to enter. ▶				28	9,425	9,263

For Paperwork Reduction Act Notice, see Form 1040 instructions. Cat. No. 12614K **Schedule A (Form 1040) 1997**

* Numbers in shaded boxes show Sally's income and its effects subtracted.

** $900 – $600 (Sally's expense) = $300 (Brad's expense).

YOUR SCHEDULE A ITEMIZED DEDUCTIONS

SCHEDULES A&B (Form 1040)

Department of the Treasury Internal Revenue Service (L)

Schedule A—Itemized Deductions

(Schedule B is on back)

► Attach to Form 1040. ► See Instructions for Schedules A and B (Form 1040).

OMB No. 1545-0074

1997

Attachment Sequence No. **07**

Name(s) shown on Form 1040 | Your social security number

Medical and Dental Expenses		*Caution: Do not include expenses reimbursed or paid by others.*				
	1	Medical and dental expenses (see page A-1)	1			
	2	Enter amount from Form 1040, line 33. [2]				
	3	Multiply line 2 above by 7.5% (.075)	3			
	4	Subtract line 3 from line 1. If line 3 is more than line 1, enter -0-			4	
Taxes You Paid (See page A-2.)	5	State and local income taxes	5			
	6	Real estate taxes (see page A-2)	6			
	7	Personal property taxes	7			
	8	Other taxes. List type and amount ►	8			
	9	Add lines 5 through 8			9	
Interest You Paid (See page A-2.)	10	Home mortgage interest and points reported to you on Form 1098	10			
	11	Home mortgage interest not reported to you on Form 1098. If paid to the person from whom you bought the home, see page A-3 and show that person's name, identifying no., and address ►	11			
Note: Personal interest is not deductible.	12	Points not reported to you on Form 1098. See page A-3 for special rules	12			
	13	Investment interest. Attach Form 4952 if required. (See page A-3.)	13			
	14	Add lines 10 through 13			14	
Gifts to Charity If you made a gift and got a benefit for it, see page A-3.	15	Gifts by cash or check. If you made any gift of $250 or more, see page A-3	15			
	16	Other than by cash or check. If any gift of $250 or more, see page A-3. You **MUST** attach Form 8283 if over $500	16			
	17	Carryover from prior year	17			
	18	Add lines 15 through 17			18	
Casualty and Theft Losses	19	Casualty or theft loss(es). Attach Form 4684. (See page A-4.)			19	
Job Expenses and Most Other Miscellaneous Deductions	20	Unreimbursed employee expenses—job travel, union dues, job education, etc. You **MUST** attach Form 2106 or 2106-EZ if required. (See page A-4.) ►	20			
	21	Tax preparation fees	21			
(See page A-5 for expenses to deduct here.)	22	Other expenses—investment, safe deposit box, etc. List type and amount ►	22			
	23	Add lines 20 through 22	23			
	24	Enter amount from Form 1040, line 33. [24]				
	25	Multiply line 24 above by 2% (.02)	25			
	26	Subtract line 25 from line 23. If line 25 is more than line 23, enter -0-			26	
Other Miscellaneous Deductions	27	Other—from list on page A-5. List type and amount ►			27	
Total Itemized Deductions	28	Is Form 1040, line 33, over $121,200 (over $60,600 if married filing separately)? **NO.** Your deduction is not limited. Add the amounts in the far right column for lines 4 through 27. Also, enter on Form 1040, line 35, the **larger** of this amount or your standard deduction. **YES.** Your deduction may be limited. See page A-5 for the amount to enter.			► 28	*

For Paperwork Reduction Act Notice, see Form 1040 instructions. Cat. No. 12614K **Schedule A (Form 1040) 1997**

★ Use revised number on Form 1040, line 35, page 100.

CHAPTER 7

POSTSCRIPT #2

CHILD-CARE TAX BENEFITS

One-income couples are probably unfamiliar with the child-care tax options. Okay, two-income couples are likely to be fuzzy on this subject, too, especially if they have relied on a paid tax preparer to do their figuring. One-income families thinking of becoming two-income families need to read the following information to find child-care tax benefits on a potential second income so tax forms can be accurately prepared. Two-incomers may want to read the following just to be sure they've made the right choices in the past.

THE CHOICES

There are two different paths to follow when claiming child-care expense. The choices are the Credit Method

and the Deduction Method (your employer must provide a dependent-care benefit through a cafeteria plan to use this second method; see pages 144–146). Occasionally, a combination of the two methods may be used, but to

Tax *credits* are often valued more highly than tax *deductions* because credits are worth their face value and subtract dollar-for-dollar from tax owed.

But tax rules monkey with expenses before transforming them into credits. Credits are always a *percentage* of the allowed expense. Thus, comparison between tax deductions (which *save* a percentage of the allowed expense) and tax credits (which *are* a percentage of the allowed expense) is a mind game.

A deduction (through an employer-provided cafeteria dependent-care account) is worth in tax savings itself times your combined federal, state, and Social Security rates. (See pages 144–146 for an explanation of cafeteria plans.) So a tax deduction under a dependent-care plan (if you're in, say, the 15 percent federal bracket and 3.35 percent state bracket plus pay 7.65 percent Social Security tax) is worth 26 percent of the allowed expense—not as good as a 30 percent credit.

Unfortunately, only low incomes qualify for the 30 percent child-care credit. The credit's percentage is reduced as income rises. Most couples receive only a 20 percent credit. But, of course, as income rises, so do tax brackets. So a deduction through a dependent-care plan (if your tax brackets and Social Security rate total 40 percent) is twice as good as a 20 percent child-care credit. As a result, the higher your income, the more likely the dependent-care deduction will save you more in taxes than the child-care credit.

keep it simple we'll treat them separately in the following boiled-down explanations.

Child and Dependent Care Expense, Form 2441, for 1040 filers (and the practically identical Schedule 2, for 1040A filers) gives steps for figuring by each method. Because 1040 and 1040A Child and Dependent Care Expense forms are so similar, everyone may use the 2441 Form that follows for evaluating the two methods. Be sure, however, to use the appropriate form and to read IRS details before filing your official tax return.

It's noteworthy that allowed expenses are not limited to child care per se. Household helpers such as cooks and housekeepers may be claimed *if* their services at least partly benefit a qualifying child under age thirteen. The catch is that there are dollar limits on work-related expense. Most taxpayers can't claim household services because their child-care expense surpasses the allowed dollar limit. Also, it's ironic that Uncle Sam says household services are not an allowed work-related expense after your youngest child becomes a teenager. This ruling implies that teenagers do the cooking and cleaning in their homes or that teenagers don't eat or clutter.

The Credit Method Parts I and II, Form 2441

Anyone can use this method. For many taxpayers it's their only choice because their employers don't offer a dependent-care benefit.

This method allows a tax *credit* of 20 to 30 percent on qualifying child-care and household services. The actual rate depends on adjusted gross income: the less earned, the higher the credit's percentage. Thus, low-income

BRAD AND SALLY'S FORM 2441 Parts I and II

Form **2441** Department of the Treasury Internal Revenue Service (O)

Child and Dependent Care Expenses

▶ Attach to Form 1040.

▶ See separate instructions.

OMB No. 1545-0068 | 1997 | Attachment Sequence No. 21

Name(s) shown on Form 1040: Bradley R. & Sally B. Smith | Your social security number: 123 00 4567

Before you begin, you need to understand the following terms. See **Definitions** on page 1 of the instructions.

- **Dependent Care Benefits**
- **Qualifying Person(s)**
- **Qualified Expenses**
- **Earned Income**

Part I **Persons or Organizations Who Provided the Care**—You **must** complete this part. (If you need more space, use the bottom of page 2.)

1 (a) Care provider's name	(b) Address (number, street, apt. no., city, state, and ZIP code)	(c) Identifying number (SSN or EIN)	(d) Amount paid (see instructions)
Bourgeois Day Care	1743 Toddler Lane Hometown, N.Y. 01040	10-7654321	6,500
Tidy-House Cleaners	4390 Lilac Lane Hometown, N.Y. 01040	11-6543217	1,440

Did you receive **dependent care benefits?** — NO → Complete only Part II below. — YES → Complete Part III on the back next.

Caution: *If the care was provided in your home, you may owe employment taxes. See the instructions for Form 1040, line 52.*

Part II **Credit for Child and Dependent Care Expenses**

2 Information about your **qualifying person(s).** If you have more than two qualifying persons, see the instructions.

(a) Qualifying person's name — First	Last	(b) Qualifying person's social security number	(c) Qualified expenses you incurred and paid in 1997 for the person listed in column (a)
Erik P.	Smith	345 00 6789	3,970
Lisa M.	Smith	456 00 7890	3,970

Line	Description		Amount
3	Add the amounts in column (c) of line 2. DO NOT enter more than $2,400 for one qualifying person or $4,800 for two or more persons. If you completed Part III, enter the amount from line 24	3	4,800
4	Enter YOUR **earned income**	4	30,000
5	If married filing a joint return, enter YOUR SPOUSE'S earned income (if student or disabled, see the instructions); **all others,** enter the amount from line 4	5	19,200 *
6	Enter the **smallest** of line 3, 4, or 5	6	4,800
7	Enter the amount from Form 1040, line 33 — 7: 49,225		
8	Enter on line 8 the decimal amount shown below that applies to the amount on line 7	8	×.20

If line 7 is— Over	But not over	Decimal amount is	If line 7 is— Over	But not over	Decimal amount is
$0	10,000	.30	$20,000	22,000	.24
10,000	12,000	.29	22,000	24,000	.23
12,000	14,000	.28	24,000	26,000	.22
14,000	16,000	.27	26,000	28,000	.21
16,000	18,000	.26	28,000	No limit	.20
18,000	20,000	.25			

Line	Description		Amount
9	Multiply **line 6** by the decimal amount on line 8. Enter the result. Then, see the instructions for the amount of credit to enter on Form 1040, line 40	9	960

For Paperwork Reduction Act Notice, see page 3 of the instructions. Cat. No. 11862M Form **2441** (1997)

* Sally's $20,000 income is reduced $800 by her retirement-plan contribution.

YOUR FORM 2441
Parts I and II

Form **2441** Department of the Treasury Internal Revenue Service (O)

Child and Dependent Care Expenses

▶ Attach to Form 1040.

▶ See separate instructions.

OMB No. 1545-0068 **1997** Attachment Sequence No. **21**

Name(s) shown on Form 1040 | Your social security number

Before you begin, you need to understand the following terms. See **Definitions** on page 1 of the instructions.

- **Dependent Care Benefits**
- **Qualifying Person(s)**
- **Qualified Expenses**
- **Earned Income**

Part I **Persons or Organizations Who Provided the Care**—You **must** complete this part. (If you need more space, use the bottom of page 2.)

1 (a) Care provider's name	(b) Address (number, street, apt. no., city, state, and ZIP code)	(c) Identifying number (SSN or EIN)	(d) Amount paid (see instructions)

Did you receive **dependent care benefits?**
- NO ⟶ Complete only Part II below.
- YES ⟶ Complete Part III on the back next.

Caution: *If the care was provided in your home, you may owe employment taxes. See the instructions for Form 1040, line 52.*

Part II **Credit for Child and Dependent Care Expenses**

2 Information about your **qualifying person(s).** If you have more than two qualifying persons, see the instructions.

(a) Qualifying person's name — First	Last	(b) Qualifying person's social security number	(c) Qualified expenses you incurred and paid in 1997 for the person listed in column (a)

3 Add the amounts in column (c) of line 2. DO NOT enter more than $2,400 for one qualifying person or $4,800 for two or more persons. If you completed Part III, enter the amount from line 24 . . . . **3**

4 Enter YOUR **earned income** **4**

5 If married filing a joint return, enter YOUR SPOUSE'S earned income (if student or disabled, see the instructions); **all others,** enter the amount from line 4 . . . . **5**

6 Enter the **smallest** of line 3, 4, or 5 . . . . **6**

7 Enter the amount from Form 1040, line 33 . . . . **7**

8 Enter on line 8 the decimal amount shown below that applies to the amount on line 7

If line 7 is— Over	But not over	Decimal amount is	If line 7 is— Over	But not over	Decimal amount is
$0—	10,000	.30	$20,000—	22,000	.24
10,000—	12,000	.29	22,000—	24,000	.23
12,000—	14,000	.28	24,000—	26,000	.22
14,000—	16,000	.27	26,000—	28,000	.21
16,000—	18,000	.26	28,000—	No limit	.20
18,000—	20,000	.25			

8 × .

9 Multiply **line 6** by the decimal amount on line 8. Enter the result. Then, see the instructions for the amount of credit to enter on Form 1040, line 40 . . . . **9**

For Paperwork Reduction Act Notice, see page 3 of the instructions. Cat. No. 11862M Form **2441** (1997) taxpayers *sometimes* get the best deal by this method. Allowable expenses are limited to $2,400 for one qualifying child (or $4,800 for two or more children).

Brad and Sally used the Credit Method for claiming child-care expense and received a federal tax credit of 20 percent ($960) and a state tax credit of 4 percent ($192) on the first $4,800 they spent. Their Form 2441, Child and Dependent Care Expenses, is on page 110. (Note: It wasn't necessary for them to list a housecleaning expense in Part I because their day-care expense was more than the allowed $4,800.)

The only jargon you need to understand to rough in your own Form 2441 is on line 4, Earned Income. Earned income for most people is wages and other compensation they report on line 7, Form 1040 or 1040A, plus net earnings from self-employment. Check instructions if you have unusual income sources.

Line 9 is an ambush which applies to a limited number of filers. Line 9 may limit the child-care credit for couples who must file the dreaded Form 6251, Alternative Minimum Tax (see page 103). These poor souls should get help. The rest of us can give thanks and continue. Unless you're caught by line 9, complete your form on page 111, using Brad and Sally's form on page 110 as a guide.

The Deduction Method
Part III, Form 2441

If your adjusted gross income is $25,000 or more, your tax savings will generally be more when using this method rather than the Credit Method—sometimes a lot more! Not everyone can use this method, though. A *cafeteria plan* with a dependent-care option must be offered through your place of employment.

Employees with this benefit are allowed to make tax-free salary-reduction contributions to special dependent-care accounts. (In other words, the contributions are *deducted* from taxable income.) Joint filers can set aside up to $5,000 per year in a dependent-care account. There is a risk, though, known as the use-it-or-lose-it rule. You forfeit any money in your account that you don't use for child-care expenses incurred during the year. So you should carefully gauge your costs.

One-child families should take special note of this method. Under the Credit Method, expenses are limited to $2,400 for one child. The dependent-care Deduction Method allows expenses up to $5,000 per year, no matter if you spend the money on one child or ten. Therefore, one-child families are more likely to be able to deduct the total cost of child care and maybe even some household services and still stay below the $5,000 limit. As an example: a one-child family qualifying for a 20 percent child-care credit would save only $480 ($2,400 × .20) on taxes. But (assuming their tax brackets and Social Security rates added up to 40 percent, and that they spent $5,000 on child-care and household services) under a dependent-care account (the Deduction Method), their tax savings would be $2,000 ($5,000 × .40).

If either Brad's or Sally's place of employment had offered a cafeteria dependent-care account, Form 2441, Child and Dependent Care Expenses, Part III, would have looked like the following form (page 114). The example shows a $5,000 contribution to a dependent-care

BRAD AND SALLY'S FORM 2441
Part III

Form 2441 (1997) Page 2

Part III **Dependent Care Benefits**

10	Enter the total amount of **dependent care benefits** you received for 1997. This amount should be shown in box 10 of your W-2 form(s). DO NOT include amounts that were reported to you as wages in box 1 of Form(s) W-2			10	5,000
11	Enter the amount forfeited, if any. See the instructions			11	-0-
12	Subtract line 11 from line 10			12	5,000
13	Enter the total amount of **qualified expenses** incurred in 1997 for the care of the **qualifying person(s)**	13	7,940		
14	Enter the **smaller** of line 12 or 13	14	5,000		
15	Enter YOUR **earned income**	15	30,000		
16	If married filing a joint return, enter YOUR SPOUSE'S earned income (if student or disabled, see the line 5 instructions); if married filing a separate return, see the instructions for the amount to enter; **all others,** enter the amount from line 15	16	19,200 *		
17	Enter the **smallest** of line 14, 15, or 16	17	5,000		
18	**Excluded benefits.** Enter here the **smaller** of the following: • The amount from line 17, or • $5,000 ($2,500 if married filing a separate return **and** you were required to enter your spouse's earned income on line 16).			18	5,000
19	**Taxable benefits.** Subtract line 18 from line 12. Also, include this amount on Form 1040, line 7. On the dotted line next to line 7, write "DCB"			19	-0-

To claim the child and dependent care credit, complete lines 20–24 below.

20	Enter $2,400 ($4,800 if two or more qualifying persons)	20	4800
21	Enter the amount from line 18	21	5000
22	Subtract line 21 from line 20. If zero or less, **STOP.** You cannot take the credit. **Exception.** If you paid 1996 expenses in 1997, see the line 9 instructions	22	-0-
23	Complete line 2 on the front of this form. DO NOT include in column (c) any excluded benefits shown on line 18 above. Then, add the amounts in column (c) and enter the total here	23	
24	Enter the **smaller** of line 22 or 23. Also, enter this amount on line 3 on the front of this form and complete lines 4–9	24	

Printed on recycled paper

★ Sally's $20,000 income is reduced $800 by her retirement-plan contribution.

YOUR FORM 2441
Part III

Part III Dependent Care Benefits

10	Enter the total amount of **dependent care benefits** you received for 1997. This amount should be shown in box 10 of your W-2 form(s). DO NOT include amounts that were reported to you as wages in box 1 of Form(s) W-2	10	
11	Enter the amount forfeited, if any. See the instructions	11	
12	Subtract line 11 from line 10	12	
13	Enter the total amount of **qualified expenses** incurred in 1997 for the care of the **qualifying person(s)**	13	
14	Enter the **smaller** of line 12 or 13	14	
15	Enter YOUR **earned income**	15	
16	If married filing a joint return, enter YOUR SPOUSE'S earned income (if student or disabled, see the line 5 instructions); if married filing a separate return, see the instructions for the amount to enter; **all others,** enter the amount from line 15	16	
17	Enter the **smallest** of line 14, 15, or 16	17	
18	**Excluded benefits.** Enter here the **smaller** of the following: • The amount from line 17, or • $5,000 ($2,500 if married filing a separate return **and** you were required to enter your spouse's earned income on line 16).	18	
19	**Taxable benefits.** Subtract line 18 from line 12. Also, include this amount on Form 1040, line 7. On the dotted line next to line 7, write "DCB"	19	

To claim the child and dependent care credit, complete lines 20–24 below.

20	Enter $2,400 ($4,800 if two or more qualifying persons)	20	
21	Enter the amount from line 18	21	
22	Subtract line 21 from line 20. If zero or less, **STOP.** You cannot take the credit. **Exception.** If you paid 1996 expenses in 1997, see the line 9 instructions	22	
23	Complete line 2 on the front of this form. DO NOT include in column (c) any excluded benefits shown on line 18 above. Then, add the amounts in column (c) and enter the total here	23	
24	Enter the **smaller** of line 22 or 23. Also, enter this amount on line 3 on the front of this form and complete lines 4–9	24	

Printed on recycled paper

account. Complete the form on page 115 for yourself, using Brad and Sally's form as a guide.

The higher your income, the more likely the deduction method through a dependent-care account will save you the most money. The catch: not all employers offer a dependent-care option. The second catch: the use-it-or-lose-it rule. (You lose money paid into the account if you don't use it during the same year you paid it.)

Compare your tax savings using the Credit Method vs. the Deduction Method by completing the worksheet, following Brad and Sally's example.

BRAD AND SALLY'S TAX COMPARISON THE CHILD-CARE CREDIT VS. THE CHILD-CARE DEDUCTION

1. Federal tax savings from child-care credit (Form 2441, page 110, line 9)	1a. $960	
State tax savings from child-care credit (from state tax return, page 123, line 20)	1b. $192	
2. Total tax savings from child-care credits (add lines 1a and 1b)		$1,152*
3. Child-care deduction (Form 2441, page 114, line 18)	$5,000	
4. Federal tax rate — 4a 15 %		
State tax rate — 4b 4.7 %		
Social Security rate — 4c 7.65%		
Total tax rate (add 4a, 4b, 4c) — 4d 27.35%		
5. Total tax savings from child-care deduction (multiply line 3 by line 4d)		$1,368*

* Compare amounts on line 2 (child-care credit tax savings) and line 5 (child-care deduction tax savings). The larger number is the better bargain.

YOUR TAX COMPARISON THE CHILD-CARE CREDIT VS. THE CHILD-CARE DEDUCTION

1. Federal tax savings from child-care credit
   (Form 2441, page 111, line 9) 1a. $______
   State tax savings from child-care credit
   (if any, from your state tax return) 1b. $______
2. Total tax savings from child-care credits
   (add lines 1a and 1b) $______*

---

3. Child-care deduction
   (Form 2441, page 115, line 18) $______
4. Federal tax rate 4a ______%
   State tax rate 4b ______%
   Social Security rate 4c ______%*
   Total tax rate
   (add 4a, 4b, 4c) 4d ______%
5. Total tax savings from child-care deduction
   (multiply line 3 by line 4d) $______**

---

* The Social Security rate is 7.65 percent for wage earners and about 12.5 percent for the self-employed (see pages 128–130 for an explanation).
** Compare amounts on line 2 (child-care credit tax savings) and line 5 (child-care deduction tax savings). The larger number is the better bargain.

8

State Income Tax

Uncle Sam has fifty little brothers (the states) who also have very healthy appetites. In most states it's an immense mistake to forget to subtract their "nib-blings" from spendable income. Brad and Sally thought state income tax would be insignificant and therefore missed a very important job-related expense.

To give state income taxes the attention and ranking they deserve, remember that Sally paid $160 per month in federal income tax and a surprising $75 in state income tax. Like their big brother, the states have a special fondness for second incomes, and they go to the same great lengths to conceal the differences in *true* tax rates between first and second incomes. Although state rates often seem kinder than federal rates, the states have learned to stir numbers just as well as their big brother—and they have the added advantage of getting to pick our brains while we're still numb from struggling through the federal maze. State income tax laws are usually not as complicated as federal laws, but many taxpayers, mentally worn after completing federal forms, glance through their state returns and never notice the gusto of their state's appetite.

State income tax rates vary widely. Seven states (Alaska, Florida, Nevada, South Dakota, Texas, Washington, and Wyoming) have no state income tax, and New Hampshire and Tennessee tax only interest and dividends. So if you live in one of these nine states, you may add a zero to the state taxes row on Your Second-Income JREs worksheet, pages 12–13, and rejoin us in chapter 9.

The other forty-one states have rates that range up to 12 percent, and each state nibbles by a different set of rules, with its own income brackets, credits, deductions,

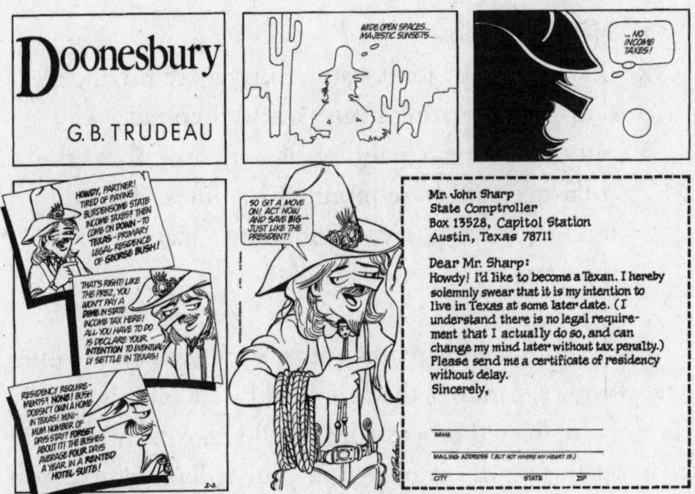

and exemption allowances. Thus, state taxable income (line 17, page 122, on Brad and Sally's return) is just as significant as tax rate—and makes comparison between states impossible based on rates alone. State taxable income also often varies a great deal from federal taxable income, making lower state rates not as benign as they appear. Brad and Sally's state taxable income was much higher than their federal taxable income, primarily because of New York's lower exemption allowance. Sally's state taxable income also included her retirement-plan contribution, and New York's child-care credit was not nearly as generous as the federal.

As with federal forms, you can avoid most rule-reading when trying to identify state income tax cost on a second income. Use the same three steps from chapter 7 to find federal tax on a second income to find state tax:

1. Hold your nose.
2. Refigure your joint state return by removing all entries originating from second income.
3. Subtract the tax paid by first income from the total tax paid by combined incomes. This difference is your second income's state income tax cost.

Even though you are unfamiliar with your state's finer tax points, separating the numbers by income is usually an uncomplicated process and should take even less time than separating the numbers on your federal return. You will need a copy of your last state income tax return and the tax computation schedule for "married, filing joint" or the tax tables in the return's instruction book. (If you've thrown away the instruction book, public libraries can often provide photocopies of the schedules and tables, even out of season, when tax materials are difficult to find at usual distribution points.)

Like the IRS, many states provide both tax schedules (similar to Schedule Y–1, page 92) and tax tables to figure out tax owed. Most states, however, require taxpayers to use tax tables until taxable income reaches a certain point, usually around $50,000 to $60,000. Still, some states provide tax schedules for all income levels so that taxpayers can identify their *official* tax rate. You may be in the look-but-don't-touch income level for your state's tax schedule, but referring to it while using the tax tables will give you a clearer view of your state's appetite. Like the federal schedules and tables, states' schedule numbers may vary by a few dollars from table numbers because the tables are generally given in fifty-dollar increments.

ADD IT UP

The following two pages show Brad and Sally's joint New York tax return and how they refigured payment by removing all entries originating from Sally's income (step 2). Use their form as an example of how to refigure your own state return.

Single-Income Couples: Using the same method as in chapter 7, single-income couples can find the cost of state income tax on a potential second income by *adding* projected second income and its effects to their state income tax return. As in the preceding three steps, the total tax difference between the two sets of numbers is the second income's estimated tax cost.

BRAD AND SALLY'S STATE TAX RETURN

New York State Department of Taxation and Finance

Resident Income Tax Return

New York State • City of New York • City of Yonkers

1997 **IT-200**

For office use only

This is a scannable form; please file this original return with the Tax Department.

Attach label, or print or type

Last name / First name and middle initial *(if joint return, enter both names)*: Smith Bradley R. & Sally B.

Your social security number: 123-00-4567

Mailing address *(number and street or rural route)*: 429 Mill Road — Apartment number

Spouse's social security number: 234-00-5678

City, village or post office / State / ZIP code: Hometown, N.Y. 01040

NY State county of residence: Albany

In the space below, print or type your permanent home address within New York State if it is **not** the same as your mailing address above *(see instructions)*.

School district name: Hometown

Permanent home address *(number and street or rural route)* — Apartment number

School district code number 999

City, village or post office — State NY — ZIP code

If taxpayer is deceased, enter first name and date of death.

(A) Filing status — mark an "X" in one box:

① ☐ Single

② ☒ Married filing joint return *(enter spouse's social security number above)*

③ ☐ Married filing separate return *(enter spouse's social security number above)*

④ ☐ Head of household *(with qualifying person)*

⑤ ☐ Qualifying widow(er) with dependent child

Staple check or money order here

(B) Did you itemize your deductions on your 1997 **federal** income tax return?... Yes ☒ No ☐

(C) Can you be claimed as a dependent on another taxpayer's federal return?... Yes ☐ No ☒

(D) If you do not need forms mailed to you next year, mark an "X" in the box *(see instructions)* .... ☐

		Line	Dollars	Cents	
1	Wages, salaries, tips, etc.	1	49,200		30,000 *
2	Taxable interest income	2	25		25
3	Dividend income	3			
4	Taxable refunds, credits or offsets of state and local income taxes *(also enter on line 12 below)*	4			
5	Unemployment compensation	5			
6	Add lines 1 through 5	6	49,225		30,025
7	Individual retirement arrangement (IRA) deduction *(see instructions)*	7			
8	Subtract line 7 from line 6. This is your **federal adjusted gross income**	8	49,225		30,025
9	Public employee contributions *(see instructions)* Identify: 414(R)	9	800	**	
10	Flexible benefits program (IRC 125 amount) *(see instructions)* Identify:	10			
11	Add lines 8, 9 and 10	11	50,025		30,025
12	Taxable refunds, credits or offsets of state and local income taxes from line 4 above	12			
13	Interest income on U.S. government bonds *(see instructions)*	13			
14	New York standard deduction *(see instructions)*	14	13,000		13,000
15	Exemptions for **dependents only** *(not the same as total federal exemptions; see instructions)*	15	2,000	00	2,000
16	Add lines 12 through 15 *(if line 16 is more than or equal to line 11, see instructions for line 17)*	16	15,000		15,000
17	Subtract line 16 from line 11. This is your **taxable income** *(if $65,000 or more, stop; you must file Form IT-201)*	17	35,025		15,025

Staple your check or money order to the front left of this return in the area indicated.

011798 — This is a scannable form; please file this original return with the Tax Department. — IT-200 1997

* Numbers in shaded boxes show Sally's income and its effects subtracted to reveal tax on Brad's income alone.
** Sally's retirement-plan contribution.

IT-200 (1997) (back)

Line	Description	Dollars	Cents
18	Enter the amount from line 17 on the front page. This is your **taxable income**	35,025	15,025
19	New York State tax on line 18 amount. *(Use the State Tax Table on tinted pages)*	1,652	601
20	New York State household credit *(from table I, II, or III; see instructions)*	-0-	35
21	Subtract line 20 from line 19 *(if line 20 is more than line 19, leave blank)*. This is the total of your New York State taxes ▶	1,652	566
22	City of New York resident tax on line 18 amount. *(Use City Tax Table on white pages)*		
23	City of New York household credit *(see instructions)*		
24	Subtract line 23 from line 22 *(if line 23 is more than line 22, leave blank)*		
25	City of New York nonresident earnings tax *(attach Form NYC-203)*		
26	City of Yonkers resident income tax surcharge *(from Yonkers Worksheet)*		
27	City of Yonkers nonresident earnings tax *(attach Form Y-203)*		
28	Add lines 24 through 27. This is the total of your city of New York and city of Yonkers taxes ▶		
29	If you want to Return a Gift to Wildlife, enter amount - $5, $10, $20, other *(see instructions)*		00
30	If you want to contribute to the Lake Placid Olympic Fund, enter $2 *($4 if your spouse **also** wants to contribute **and** you are filing jointly. See instructions)*		00
31	If you want to give a Gift for Breast Cancer Research and Education, enter amount - $5, $10, $20, other *(see instructions)*		00
32	If you want to contribute to the Missing and Exploited Children Clearinghouse Fund, enter amount - $5, $10, $20, other *(see instructions)*		00
33	Add lines 21, 28, 29, 30, 31, and 32	1,652	566
34	New York State child and dependent care credit *(from Form IT-216; attach form)*	192	-0-
35	New York State earned income credit *(from Form IT-215; attach form)*		
36	Real property tax credit *(from Form IT-214, line 17; attach form)*		
37	Total New York State tax withheld *(staple wage and tax statements; see instructions)*	2,025	1,095
38	Total city of New York tax withheld *(staple wage and tax statements; see instructions)*		
39	Total city of Yonkers tax withheld *(staple wage and tax statements; see instructions)*		
40	Add lines 34 through 39	2,217	1,095*
41	**If line 40 is more than line 33,** subtract line 33 from line 40. This is the amount to be **refunded to you**	565	529*
42	**If line 40 is less than line 33,** subtract line 40 from line 33. This is the **amount you owe** *(do not send cash; make your check or money order payable to **New York State Income Tax**; write your social security number and **1997 income tax** on it)*		*

1,652
− 192
$1,460 Total TAX Column one

• Staple your wage and tax statements at the top of the back of this return. See Step 7, for the proper assembly of your return and attachments.

The important numbers!

If you choose to have your refund sent directly to your bank account, complete a, b, and c below *(see instructions)*.

a Routing number
b Type: Checking Savings
c Account number

Paid Preparer's Use Only — Preparer's signature; Date; Mark "X" if self-employed; Firm's name *(or yours, if self-employed)*; Preparer's social security number; Address; Employer identification number

Sign Your Return Here — Your signature: Bradley R. Smith; Spouse's signature *(if joint return)*: Sally B. Smith; Date: 4/20/98; Daytime phone number (optional) ( )

012798

This is a scannable form; please file this original return with the Tax Department.
Mail to: STATE PROCESSING CENTER, PO BOX 61000, ALBANY NY 12261-0001

IT-200 1997

* Ignore. Amounts withheld, owed, or to be refunded have nothing to do with how much your tax was, except that their differences *sometimes* reveal the tax paid.

City Income or Earnings Tax: If you get hit a third time by a city tax, include city tax numbers with state tax totals.

Déjà vu. Just as in chapter 7, you're now ready for step 3, calculating your second income's true tax cost: *Subtract tax paid by first income from tax paid by combined incomes* (the difference between numbers on the line showing total tax owed). *Then divide by 12 for monthly cost.*

BRAD AND SALLY'S FIGURES

$1,460	–	$566	=	$894	÷ 12 =	$75
Tax on combined incomes		Tax on first income		Tax on second income		Monthly JRE on second income

As with the federal figures, true or effective state tax rates for second incomes are usually much higher than for first incomes. Sally earned only 40 percent of their total income, but her earnings accounted for 61 percent ($894 ÷ $1,460) of their combined state tax bill!

YOUR FIGURES

$_____	–	$_____	=	$_____	÷ 12 =	$_____ *
Tax on combined incomes		Tax on first income		Tax on second income		Monthly JRE on second income

* ENTER this number as a negative on the state taxes row on Your Second-Income JREs worksheet, pages 12–13.

9

Social Security

Uncle Sam returns for a generous dessert after he and his little brothers enjoy their meals in chapters 7 and 8. This last bite is called the Social Security tax, a.k.a. FICA, or self-employment tax when applied to self-employed workers. Because the money is so silently sliced from incomes, it often goes unrecognized that many workers pay more Social Security tax than federal income tax!

Teenagers examining their first paychecks invariably ask, "What the ★²#§ is FICA?"; adults are still asking the same question. FICA stands for Federal Insurance Contribution Act, the law that authorized Social Security payroll deductions. To confuse us, the term FICA is often used to mean Social Security.

Social Security now includes not only retirement, but also disability and survivors' benefits plus hospital insur-

1998 SOCIAL SECURITY AND MEDICARE TAX RATES FOR WAGE EARNERS

If gross salary is over—	But not over—	Tax is	Of amount over—
$0	$68,400	7.65%★	$0
$68,400		$5,232.60	
		+1.45%★★	$68,400

★ 6.2 percent Social Security plus 1.45 percent Medicare tax.
★★ Medicare tax.

1998 SELF-EMPLOYMENT AND MEDICARE TAX RATES FOR THE SELF-EMPLOYED

If self-employed income × .9235 is over—	But not over—	Tax is	Of amount over—
$0★	$68,400	15.3%★★	$0
$68,400		$10,465.20	
		+2.9%†	$68,400

★ If less than $400 you do not owe self-employment tax.
★★ 12.4 percent self-employment plus 2.9 percent Medicare tax.
† Medicare tax.

ance (Medicare). Accordingly, the Social Security (and Medicare) tax has increased along with expanded benefits. When Social Security was first enacted in 1937, workers paid 1 percent on maximum yearly earnings of

$3,000. Increases have been the norm for the last few decades. In 1998, workers pay 7.65 percent (15.3 percent if self-employed) on maximum earnings of $68,400; and an additional 1.45 percent (2.9 percent if self-employed) Medicare tax on earnings above $68,400.

The preceding schedules expose why the Social Security tax is such a large job-related expense. Many workers pay more in Social Security tax than in federal income tax because *all* income is taxed. That is, all income except (wouldn't you know there'd be an except) contributions to cafeteria plans (see pages 144–146), and two paltry deductions for the self-employed, discussed later. It's also important to note that separate Social Security accounts are maintained for every worker. Spouses cannot combine incomes for the purpose of paying Social Security tax. A husband and wife *each* earning wages of $68,400 will *both* pay the 7.65 percent rate, generally, on total earnings.

ADD IT UP

Wage earners may think they're getting a half-price rate when they compare their rates to those of self-employed workers (7.65 percent vs. 15.3 percent). Strictly speaking, though, Social Security taxes everyone at the 15.3 percent rate. Many employees are unaware that their employers must match their Social Security contributions dollar for dollar, in effect, doubling their 7.65 percent rate to 15.3 percent. Although your employer's dollar match does not directly come out of your pocket, it does affect the moneys available for wage increases.

Wage Earners

If you have last year's W–2 Wage and Tax Statement, or your final December pay stub from last year, you may skip the math. Notice, however, that Social Security and Medicare taxes are separated on W–2s (usually boxes 4 and 6), and should be combined for total tax withheld. If you're referring to a pay stub, the numbers may already be combined and listed under either FICA or Social Security.

If you can't find last year's W–2 or your last pay stub, you can use the schedule for wage earners on page 126 to estimate Social Security (and Medicare) tax paid. (Be sure you subtract contributions to cafeteria accounts from gross income before figuring tax.)

Single-Income Couples: Single-income couples can find Social Security tax on a potential second income by using the wage earner's schedule on page 126.

To find monthly Social Security tax JREs, divide year's total Social Security (and Medicare) tax by 12 (months). Use the worksheet following Sally's on the next page.

The Self-Employed

With Social Security self-employment rates at 15.3 percent, a diversion has become necessary so that the self-employed don't organize some sort of tax revolt. So now, (hold on to your pencil) the self-employed are:

1. Required to pay self-employment (Social Security) tax on only 92.35 percent of self-employed income (see self-employment schedule, page 126). This lowers the rate to 14.13 percent rather than 15.3 percent. The Social Security tax rate-makers didn't use 14.13 percent

SALLY'S FIGURES

$1,530	÷	12	=	$128
Social Security (and Medicare) tax				Monthly Social Security JRE

YOUR FIGURES

$______	÷	12	=	$______★
Social Security (and Medicare) tax				Monthly Social Security JRE

★ ENTER this number as a negative on the Social Security row on Your Second-Income JREs worksheet, pages 12–13.

at the start because the self-employed wouldn't have liked 14.13 percent much better than 15.3 percent.

2. Allowed to deduct one-half of self-employment tax from adjusted gross income (line 26, Form 1040). Voilà, one of Uncle Sam's best smoke and mirror tricks! Although this sounds like the tax is being cut in half, this deduction only reduces the above 14.13 percent rate to around 12 or 13 percent, depending on your tax bracket.

If your self-employed second income was included on last year's tax return, your self-employment tax is included in line 53, total tax. This doesn't mean you didn't pay self-employment tax; it's just lumped together with income tax owed, making it harder to identify the tax value of the above two tax "breaks." Add a zero to the Social Security row on Your Second-Income JREs worksheet, pages 12–13. Remember, though, you did pay it (in chapter 7).

The self-employed clearly have a bigger direct tax bite than wage earners. If you're self-employed (whether designing skyscrapers or baby-sitting) the Social Security tax JRE can be a significant setback to a viable spendable income.

Single-Income Couples: Single-income couples can estimate Social Security cost of a potential self-employed second income by one of two methods:

1. Be sure you included cost of and deduction for self-employment tax on Form 1040 (lines 26 and 47) (chapter 7), when you figured tax cost on two incomes (see note, page 102). If you did, self-employment tax is included in total tax owed (line 53). Add a zero to the Social Security row on Your Second-Income JREs worksheet, pages 12–13. Remember, though, you did pay it (in chapter 7).

2. Chances are, however, you missed including the self-employment tax on Form 1040. To save redoing Form 1040, multiply projected self-employed income by 12.5 percent to find approximate tax. (See pages 128–129 for why you're multiplying by 12.5 percent.) Divide the result by 12 (months), and add the result to the Social Security row on Your Second-Income JREs worksheet, pages 12–13.

WHAT ABOUT RETIREMENT BENEFITS??

Married couples should consider the long-term effects on retirement income if one spouse has contributed little to the Social Security system. The consequences are not as dire as you may expect.

Social Security retirement benefits are usually based on average lifetime work record or earnings. But, spouses also can draw on husbands' or wives' accounts without ever contributing to the system. Generally, at age sixty-five, a spouse, with no work record of his or her own, can receive a benefit equal to half of the other spouse's benefit. And a widower's or widow's benefit (if married at least nine months) can be as much as 100 percent of the deceased's benefit. (Divorced spouses or divorced widows or widowers must have been married at least ten years in order to collect benefits from a former spouse's account.) *There are exceptions to these rules, so check with the Social Security Administration about your particular circumstances.*

Women are more likely than men to not work continuously, and overall they earn only about 73 cents for every dollar their husbands earn. Thus, their Social Security contributions under their own account may not increase retirement benefits. At retirement age, many wives with irregular or low earnings discover their Social Security benefit under their husband's account is higher than their own account's benefit. In other words, their contributions through the years have not increased their retirement benefits! Many more women find the difference in benefits, between their own accounts versus drawing on their husband's account, to be negligible—and no justification for the amount of money they have paid into the system.

It wouldn't be smart to plan your golden years based on the above generalities, though, because the rules are complicated. To receive a personal and detailed estimate of retirement benefits, call Social Security (1-800-772-

1213) and request a *Personal Earnings and Benefit Estimate Statement* (*PEBES*) for both you and your spouse. The *PEBES* is interesting reading and would be worth paying for—but, it's *free!* Anyone serious about retirement planning should be picking up the phone *now.*

After studying your *PEBES,* you should investigate the magic of time and compound interest. A small private investment program could easily make up for any shortfall in total benefits for one spouse drawing only on the other's account. Notice in the following table the importance of time and interest rates.

INTEREST RATES

$50 per month compounded daily

Years	6%	9%	12%
10	$8,242	$9,767	$11,657
20	$23,258	$33,786	$50,353
30	$50,618	$92,857	$178,802
40	$100,469	$238,132	$605,182

NOTE: Under a tax-deductible plan, tax savings (in the 28 percent bracket) would result in a true cost of $36 per month.

Beginning at age twenty-five, a couple saving $50 per month in a tax-sheltered plan earning 9 percent interest could have $238,132 at the end of forty years. Then, if principal were never touched, interest at the same 9 percent could produce income of at least $1,786 per month ($238,132 × .09 ÷ 12) for them, then their children, then their grandchildren . . . *forever.*

10
Deductible Job Expenses

Adults trust in Uncle Sam to deliver tax deductions the way children believe in Santa Claus and the Tooth Fairy. Our children would surely notice if their Christmas stockings were empty or no coins replaced their missing teeth under their pillows. Yet, we adults hardly ever check on Uncle Sam's much-touted deductible job-expense "gifts." If we did, we'd often be disappointed.

WHAT'S A JOB-EXPENSE DEDUCTION WORTH? (PROBABLY NOT MUCH)

Tax-deductions for employee expenses usually disappear up Uncle Sam's sleeve by way of one of his best now-you-see-it, now-you-don't tricks. Sally had $600 and Brad had $300 in deductible employee expenses—and they naively thought Uncle Sam picked up their bill! Furthermore, when their thoughts were on taxes, they also believed that somehow the same deductible expenses resulted in a tax savings. If Brad and Sally had paid close attention to what happened on Schedule A, page 105, they would have recognized Sally's $600 as a job-related expense which they paid without tax relief.

TAX DEDUCTIONS ARE NEVER WORTH THEIR FACE VALUE AND SOMETIMES WORTH NOTHING! Tax deductions subtract from federal (and usually state) taxable income—but not directly from tax owed. Thus, a deduction's real value is generally worth itself times your combined federal and state rates; the higher your rates (and income), the more valuable your deductions. A $100 deduction in the 15 percent federal bracket and in the 4 percent state bracket is worth $19 ($100 × .19) in tax savings. The same deduction in the 31 percent federal bracket and 10 percent state bracket is worth $41 ($100 × .41).

Brad and Sally's combined incomes fell into the 15 percent federal bracket and 4.7 percent state bracket. Knowing this, Sally's $600 deduction *appears* to be worth $118 ($600 × .197). But employee job-expense deductions must go through the now-you-see-it, now-you-don't program. As they move toward Uncle Sam's sleeve they're reduced by 2 percent of Adjusted Gross Income (line 33, Form 1040). Brad and Sally's combined AGI was $49,225. Their combined employee expenses of $900 were reduced to *nothing* ($49,225 × .02 = $985; Schedule A, page 105, line 26). The Tooth Fairy would get bit if she made deliveries like this.

Marcy and Rich (chapters 1, 4, and 7) got an even worse deal than Brad and Sally. Marcy *had* a $1,200 job-expense deduction, which was wiped out with Rich's income added to their AGI. When Rich quit work, she got the deduction back.

WHAT'S DEDUCTIBLE? (PROBABLY NOT MUCH)

Uncle Sam devotes many exhausting pages defining and limiting deductible employee expenses. Most of us are somewhat familiar with what is and isn't allowed for our particular occupations and don't want to read fine points for seaweed harvesters and astronauts. The list on page 138 is by no means complete, nor does it enumerate requirements and limitations that apply to the separate listings. In short, be careful when reading rules that apply to your employee deductions. Uncle Sam is very fussy about deductible employee expenses and has visited (audited) many nieces and nephews regarding questionable deductions.

Be sure to note that deductible clothing must *not* be suitable for everyday use. This means a nurse's uniform is usually deductible, but a business suit generally isn't because you might wear it off-hours. Include nondeductible clothing needed to maintain a presentable appearance in your job under personal upkeep (chapter 2).

cathy® by Cathy Guisewite

Transportation, meals, and entertainment costs, *if a part of your job,* are generally deductible. (Meals and entertainment, however, are subject to a 50 percent limitation.) Commuting expense and regular meals during work hours are not deductible; include them under transportation, lunches, and coffee breaks (chapter 3).

Moreover, you may not meet requirements to claim a sometimes deductible expense, such as a home office. If you are not allowed to declare the expense, the cost should be listed later in chapter 12, And What Else?

cathy® by Cathy Guisewite

ADD IT UP

Sally had deductible expenses for professional dues and license renewal costs of $145 and $90 respectively. Plus, to keep her social worker's license current, she had $365 in education expense her first year.

On the following page, list your qualifying job expenses, even if you did not itemize or receive a deduction for them on Schedule A. Don't include expenses reimbursed by your employer. But, if an allowed deduction was limited (such as the 50 percent limit on meals and entertainment), record your total outlay.

Smoke and mirrors can get in the way here. If you had a deduction for job expense on Schedule A, line 26, its value (if any) reduced tax owed. The worth of the deduction can't be subtracted twice. Perhaps it did save money on taxes, but its value can't also be subtracted in this chapter from job expense. Thus, your total outlay for deductible job expense should be listed in this chapter as a JRE.

Single-Income Couples: Single-income couples have two options for finding the potential tax savings of their estimated deductible job expenses:

1. Assume the deduction is worth nothing (which it probably is). Complete the Deductible Job Expense worksheet on the following page using your best estimate of deductible job expenses for projected second income. Enter the total as a negative in the row for deductible job expense on Your Second-Income JREs worksheet, pages 12–13.

2. Go back to chapter 7 and refigure Schedule A using your best estimate of deductible job expenses for pro-

DEDUCTIBLE JOB EXPENSE ($)

	Sally's Expenses	Your Expenses
1. Transportation	______	______
2. Meals and entertainment	______	______
3. Liability or malpractice insurance	______	______
4. Safety equipment, tools, supplies	______	______
5. Uniforms and work clothes	______	______
6. Medical exams	______	______
7. Union and professional dues	145	______
8. Subscriptions to trade and professional journals	______	______
9. Job search expense	______	______
10. Home office	______	______
11. Education	365	______
12. Other	90	______
Total deductible job expense	$600 ÷ 12 =	______ ÷ 12 =
Monthly deductible job expense	$50	______ ★

★ ENTER this number as a negative on the deductible job expense row on Your Second-Income JREs worksheet, pages 12–13.

jected second income. Then, redo your Form 1040 and state form, using your revised itemized deductions. Accordingly, change the tax owed in the rows for federal and state taxes on pages 12–13. Then, complete the Deductible Job Expense worksheet above using your estimated deductible job expenses. Enter that result as a negative in the deductible job expense row, pages 12–13. (All this trouble is necessary only for those who still believe in the Tooth Fairy.)

Self-Employed Business Expense: Self-employed people should include their business expenses on Schedule C, Profit or Loss from Business, or Schedule C-EZ, Net Profit from Business, rather than on Schedule A. A self-employed business expense usually provides greater tax savings than an employee job expense because it is not subject to the 2 percent AGI reduction or Social Security tax. Self-employed taxable income is based on net profit (gross profit minus deductible expenses). Therefore, it isn't necessary to list business expenses as JREs. Enter zero on the deductible job expense row, on Your Second-Income JREs worksheet, pages 12–13.

11

Perks or Employee Benefits

Other than earnings, the sole positive influence on spendable income for a second incomer is usually perks or employee fringe benefits. Indeed, a good fringe benefit package has become as important as salary to many employees and can save thousands of dollars that otherwise would subtract from spendable income. Unfortunately, benefit packages sometimes have false bottoms. Surprisingly, some can even reduce spendable income and are, in truth, job-related expenses in disguise.

Job perks run the gamut from free coffee to paid health insurance. They include free or discounted company products; retirement plans; life, health, dental, and disability insurance; company cars; meals; child care; country-club memberships; free parking; fitness programs; sporting event tickets; and more. Still, what is of benefit to one employee may be worthless to another. Paid health insurance means nothing to an employee who is covered under a spouse's plan. An on-site child-care facility is a waste for a childless employee.

Confusing the value of fringe benefits even further is that benefits can be

1. Taxable, or
2. Tax-deductible, or
3. Free from tax influences.

A jumble of rules governs very wavy lines drawn among taxable, nontaxable, and deductible benefits. With tax angles raising and lowering the value of benefits, it's easy to get lost in the tax maze and assume a perk or benefit to be worth its face value. You've already reflected the tax influences of your benefits in chapters 7, 8, and 9, so be sure not to subtract or add them to your benefits' values in this chapter. Yet it's important to understand tax effects on benefits' dollar worth, especially future benefits not included on tax returns in chapters 7 and 8.

Even without tax influences, a fringe benefit's value can vary among workers, making benefit evaluation a solitary consideration. Never accept a coworker's opinion of a benefit's merit. A FRINGE BENEFIT'S TRUE VALUE CAN BE FOUND BY SUBTRACTING *your* COST FOR THE BENEFIT FROM WHAT *you* WOULD HAVE OTHERWISE SPENT ON THE SAME SERVICE WITHOUT YOUR EMPLOYER'S SUPPORT.

TAXABLE AND NONTAXABLE FRINGE BENEFITS

A mishmash of tax laws defines the differences between taxable and nontaxable fringe benefits. Fortunately, however, employers are required to include taxable benefits in box 1 (wages, tips, other compensation) on W–2 Wage and Tax Statements. So, most rule reading has been done for you by your employer. Be forewarned, though, a taxable fringe benefit's value will be added to box 1 on your W–2 and thus add to your taxable income. You could end up paying not only federal and state income tax, but *also* Social Security tax on the benefit's worth! As a result, spendable income can be reduced by a "benefit," such as a health-club membership in which you may have little or no interest. Yet you may not notice the benefit's hidden cost within the tangle of numbers on your tax forms.

A $1,000 *taxable* fringe benefit will generally cost a taxpayer in the 28 percent federal bracket and 4.35 state bracket $400 in taxes (28 + 4.35 + 7.65 Social Security = 40 percent). The following examples, on page 143, illustrate the employees' costs of taxable health-club programs in which health-conscious employers enroll all employees. In example 1, the benefit costs a diehard, uninterested couch potato $33 per month. The couch potato would never have spent her own money on a health club (column 1), but because the $1,000 was added to her taxable income, her taxes increased $400 (column 2).

Example 2 illustrates the benefit's value to an employee in the same tax brackets who was spending $1,000 of his own money at a health club (column 1); thus, the benefit saved him $50 per month.

EFFECT ON SPENDABLE INCOME OF A TAXABLE FRINGE BENEFIT

	Stay-at-Home Cost		Cost with Second-Income Fringe Benefit		Cost or Value of Benefit				Monthly Perk (+) or JRE (–)
1.	$0	–	$400	=	–$400	÷	12 months	=	–$33 JRE
2.	$1,000	–	$400	=	$600	÷	12 months	=	$50 perk

On the other hand, if the health-club program qualifies as nontaxable, its dollar value could be figured as follows:

EFFECT ON SPENDABLE INCOME OF A NONTAXABLE FRINGE BENEFIT

	Stay-at-Home Cost		Cost with Second-Income Fringe Benefit		Cost or Value of Benefit				Monthly Perk (+) or JRE (–)
3.	$0	–	$0	=	$0	÷	12 months	=	$0
4.	$1,000	–	$0	=	$1,000	÷	12 months	=	$83 perk

Example 3 shows the value of a *nontaxable* health-club membership to the example 1 couch potato. With no tax expense, the couch potato breaks even on cost. Example 4 shows the benefit's true value to the employee from the second example if the health-club membership is nontaxable.

The preceding examples illustrate how the same benefit's value can vary between workers, even within the same tax bracket, with different needs and interests. A fringe benefit isn't always worth its face value, nor does it always have the same value among coworkers.

Your employer should have included your taxable benefits in your taxable income. Thus, resulting taxes are included in chapters 7, 8, and 9. It's necessary, however, to understand the tax angles if you are trying to gauge the value of a future fringe benefit.

THE CAFETERIA DEDUCTION

Even if you don't itemize deductions (Schedule A, Form 1040), you may have certain benefits that are deducted from wages (box 1 on your W–2 Wage and Tax Statement) and thus lower your tax bill. Retirement-plan contributions are sometimes deducted. Most notable, though, is the often misunderstood cafeteria plan deduction, which is invisible on tax returns.

Workers often can't agree on which perks they most want, and in an effort to please everyone, many employers are now offering "cafeteria" benefit packages. *Don't stop reading because you don't intend to eat in the company cafeteria!* Cafeteria plans have nothing to do with eating, except indirectly, because they leave you with more money to spend on food!

Cafeteria plans wear many hats, which may be why so many workers have trouble understanding them. One cafeteria plan may be referred to as a flexible-spending account or arrangement; another may be called a flexible-benefit plan or program. Still another may dub itself a dependent-care reimbursement account.

Employees with a cafeteria plan can choose the benefits most relevant to their own lives and make tax-free salary-reduction contributions to special spending accounts. Some employers also add money which they have designated for employee benefits to these accounts. Contributions help pay for nontaxable expenses such as health, life, and disability insurance; medical bills; and dependent care. (Cash also may be a cafeteria option, although it is taxable.) A salary reduction under a cafeteria plan is *deducted* from total income before it is recorded on your W–2, box 1. From there on, the deduction becomes invisible and doesn't show up on your tax return at all. Most people like to *see* their tax deductions, so they have a difficult time believing in a tax deduction they can't see.

Nevertheless, good things happen here. Recall from page 134, a deduction is generally worth itself times your combined federal and state rates in tax savings. Thus, a $100 deduction in the 31 percent federal bracket and 12 percent state bracket is usually worth $43 ($100 × .43) in tax savings. But cafeteria plan deductions are better! Because they are deducted from income *before* Social Security tax is paid, they save an additional 7.65 percent. This means upper-income brackets can save more than 50 percent (for example, 36 + 12 + 7.65) with invisible cafeteria deductions—and the rest of us don't do so badly either. Say you're in the 28 percent federal bracket and 4.35 state bracket, and of course you pay 7.65 percent Social Security tax. A $1,000 cafeteria plan contribution thus costs you in real dollars only $600 ($1,000 × .40 = $400 tax savings) per year.

Your cafeteria plan contributions should have been deducted from income before reaching your tax return. Thus, their tax savings were reflected in chapters 7, 8, and 9. Don't subtract tax savings again in this chapter unless you are evaluating cost under an anticipated cafeteria option.

HEALTH AND DENTAL INSURANCE

A national health-care plan would change the value of most workers' health benefits. The debate could come up again—and perhaps never be resolved. You can use the following information to evaluate a second income's health plan, no matter how it's delivered.

The high cost of private health insurance makes group benefit plans so attractive that employees often choose them over wage increases. If you have a health problem, you may find this benefit worth more than your salary! On the other hand, a health insurance benefit means little if it simply duplicates coverage under a spouse's health benefit. (Most policies have nonduplication-of-benefits provisions, which prevent collecting twice for the same medical expense.) Many employers provide single-person health plans and require that employees pay extra for family coverage. Because companies generally offer a choice of only single or family plans, whether you need coverage for a spouse or a spouse and twelve kids, you'll usually pay the same family rate.

Of course, evaluating insurance policies solely by cost can be a grave mistake. One plan may pay everything; another, only for surgery on a second left foot. Before deciding on the cheaper policy, compare maximum benefits, deductibles, copayments, kinds and length of treatments covered, and job security of both wage earners.

Try to keep comparisons simple! Recall, A FRINGE BENEFIT'S TRUE VALUE CAN BE FOUND BY SUBTRACTING *your* COST FOR THE BENEFIT FROM WHAT *you* WOULD HAVE OTHERWISE SPENT ON THE SAME SERVICE WITHOUT YOUR EMPLOYER'S SUPPORT. In the following five examples, I'm assuming that the health plans involved have nearly equal benefits, or that increased benefits under the more expensive plan will offset the extra cost.

In example 1 (see page 148), Brad and Sally each had employer-paid single-person health plans. To cover the children, Brad paid a $150 family-plan premium (which also covered Sally). Sally's fringe plan cost an extra $200 for family coverage. Because the two policies were nearly identical, they chose Brad's plan.

Example 2 shows one of Brad's coworkers and his wife, who each had employer-paid single-person health plans. They had no children. Without the wife's job and health plan, they would have had to add the $150 family plan to the husband's policy so they would both have coverage.

Example 3 applies to Brad and Sally's neighbors. They had no health benefits and were forced to pay $450 per month for a nongroup plan. When the wife returned to work, their cost dropped to $200 for family coverage under her company's group health plan.

EFFECT ON SPENDABLE INCOME OF A SECOND INCOME'S HEALTH INSURANCE BENEFIT

	Stay-at-Home Cost		Monthly Cost With Second-Income Fringe Benefit		Monthly Perk (+) or JRE (–)
1.	$150	–	$200	=	$0⋆
2.	$150	–	$0	=	$150 perk
3.	$450	–	$200	=	$250 perk
4.	$600	–	$200	=	$400 perk
5.	$3,000	–	$200	=	$2,800 perk

⋆ ENTER 0 when results are negative. It's assumed that you will enroll in the cheaper health plan or that the increased benefits under the more expensive plan will offset extra cost.

Example 4 is a revision of example 3. The neighbors reevaluated their expenses with their old policy when they learned the wife's new dental rider would pay $150 per month toward the cost of their children's braces. They added the $150 to column 1 ($450 + $150 = $600) to reflect a more accurate view of their expenses with the old policy. (Add medical bills only when increased benefits under the other policy are *substantial,* and you are *sure* you will receive them.)

In example 5, because of their age and the husband's poor health, this couple paid $3,000 per *month* in health insurance premiums. *Yes,* this really happens! Luckily, the wife found work that offered family coverage for $200 per month. Her benefit was worth $2,800 ($3,000 – $200) monthly—making her salary a secondary issue!

NOTE: If you paid your health insurance premium through a cafeteria plan, your payments were deducted from income before they reached your tax return. So your tax savings were reflected in chapters 7, 8, and 9. Don't subtract tax savings in this chapter unless you are gauging cost under a future cafeteria option.

RETIREMENT PLANS

Retirement plans pose special problems when figuring spendable income. No one, not even the most qualified financial expert, can do more than estimate the dollar value of a retirement plan because its final value hinges on your life span and the success of investments under the plan. Considering that you won't realize these benefits until retirement, their value in terms of your current income is nil. And because most retirement plans require employee contributions, they also reduce your current spendable income. This is not to say you shouldn't plan for retirement, but here I'm focusing on determining *current* spendable income.

In Sally's case, she and her employer each contributed $67 per month to her retirement plan. Considering Sally was facing financial and emotional disaster because of the breakup of her marriage, the advantages of extra retirement income didn't outweigh her current problems. Before the divorce, retirement income seemed a bad bargain for Sally if it was her only real benefit from working. Financial counselors will tear up their spreadsheets at this reasoning, so let's reemphasize the importance of retirement planning. Yet, for everything there is a season. In many cases, it might be better to begin a private investment program (as explained on page 132) or postpone retirement planning until the second paycheck is more productive.

The first example below illustrates the influence of Sally's $67-per-month retirement-fund contribution on her spendable income. Because she had no intention of contributing to a retirement plan, her mandatory contribution resulted in a subtraction of $67 per month from her current spendable income.

EFFECT ON SPENDABLE INCOME OF A COMPANY RETIREMENT PLAN

	Stay-at-Home Cost		Monthly Cost With Second-Income Fringe Benefit		Monthly Perk (+) or JRE (–)
1.	$0	–	$67	=	–$67 JRE
2.	$134	–	$67	=	$67 perk

The second example shows the effect a company retirement plan could have on spendable income for a worker who would otherwise have paid into a private plan. She listed in column 1 the cost of a private retirement plan of roughly the same value as the company plan which cost her $67 in column 2. (Her employer matched dollar for dollar her contributions in column 2, so she gauged a private plan of near value would cost twice the company plan.) Thus, her company retirement plan benefit resulted in a $67 perk or addition to spendable income.

NOTE: If your retirement plan contribution was subtracted from income on your W–2, tax savings were shown in chapters 7, 8, and 9. Don't subtract tax savings in this chapter unless you are estimating the cost of a future retirement plan.

FREE OR DISCOUNTED MERCHANDISE

Many businesses offer employees free or discounted merchandise or services that they sell to the public. This is a gloomy benefit if you work in a casket factory, but a very exciting one if you work for an airline. Some employees are their company's best customers. A ten-year-old working in a candy store will develop a terrific craving for candy and let a 20 percent employee discount justify his purchases. We adults aren't much better than our children—although casket company employees may be exceptions to this rule.

A computer saleswoman, lured by an employee discount, can get caught in her own sales pitch and begin to believe that she must own the best of what she sells. The chart on page 152 illustrates three different ways the same computer purchased with a nontaxable discount could be calculated as an addition to (perk) or subtraction from (JRE) spendable income. Remember, A FRINGE BENEFIT'S TRUE VALUE IS FOUND BY SUBTRACTING *your* COST FOR THE BENEFIT FROM WHAT *you* WOULD HAVE OTHERWISE SPENT ON THE SAME SERVICE WITHOUT YOUR EMPLOYER'S SUPPORT.

Tax laws go round and round about the differences between taxable and nontaxable, free and discounted merchandise. *Generally,* discounts are nontaxable if they are not more than the employer's gross profit percentage. Free services are usually nontaxable if the employer does not incur substantial additional cost in providing the benefit. (For example, free standby airline tickets are generally nontaxable; reserved seat tickets are generally taxable.) On the other hand, if free or discounted merchandise is offered only to top-brass employees, the benefit's value is taxable.

EFFECT ON SPENDABLE INCOME OF A NONTAXABLE EMPLOYEE DISCOUNT

	Stay-at-Home Cost		Cost with Second-Income Fringe Benefit		Cost or Value of Benefit				Monthly Perk (+) or JRE (–)
1.	$5,000	–	$3,500	=	$1,500	÷	12 months	=	$125 perk
2.	$1,700	–	$3,500	=	–$1,800	÷	12 months	=	–$150 JRE
3.	$ 0	–	$3,500	=	–$3,500	÷	12 months	=	–$292 JRE

Computer 1 was purchased by an employee who had definitely planned to spend $5,000 on a computer system before she began working at the computer store. Because she saved $1500 with her employee discount, the $1500 savings results in a perk or addition to spendable income.

Computer 2 was purchased by an employee who had also planned to buy a computer before he began working at the computer store. However, he had budgeted only $1,700 on a cheaper (but just as good for his needs) system, but ended up spending $3,500 instead. His "discount" cost him $1,800.

Computer 3 was purchased by an impressionable employee who never wanted or needed a computer before she began working in the computer store. She bought the computer, used it for a month, then let it collect dust. Because she would have spent nothing on a computer before employment, and she spent $3,500 after, her discount cost her $3,500.

OTHER PERKS (AND JREs)

Allison, a junior executive with an airline, had the impressive fringe benefits listed in the table on page 155. Explanations of each benefit's real dollar value or cost precede and follow Allison's list. The tax note at the end of each explanation is meant to provide as much information as possible without causing you to mislay your pencil. You'll need to get more comprehensive information for doing anything official, like filing a tax return.

In the interest of fair play, I should point out that in certain cases you may not *have* to read the tax notes. When looking for the value of a *future* benefit that was not included on your last tax return, read the tax notes and adjust the numbers accordingly. When looking for the value of a *past* benefit that was included on your last tax return, you may ignore the tax notes. Tax influences were reflected in your taxes in chapters 7, 8, and 9, and shouldn't be added or subtracted again in this chapter.

Reading the tax notes, however, will give you a better picture of what your fringe benefits are doing for you—or to you—inside the tangle of numbers on your tax returns. I've included the tax influences of Allison's benefit list in the table on the next page to give a clear view of her benefit package's real worth.

Allison's benefit package had major leaks. All totaled, her "benefits" reduced her spendable income by $290 per month! To be sure, some of her benefits were quite enjoyable, but their hidden costs took away from redecorating her dream house, her foremost financial goal. The leaks in her benefit package weren't the only reason Allison's income vanished, but they were contributing accomplices along with JREs in other chapters. The following closer look at Allison's benefits shows why most aren't a plus to her spendable income and will help you evaluate your own benefits.

1. *Health Insurance:* Allison's husband, Michael, paid $125 per month for his employer's excellent insurance plan, which covered their entire family (column 1). The airline policy covered Allison but required a $190-per-month contribution (column 2) for a family plan. The plans were nearly identical, so they chose Michael's policy.

TAX NOTE: If Allison's health insurance had been included in a cafeteria plan (pages 144–146), her $190 cost would have been reduced by her combined official income tax and Social Security rates (28 percent federal, 8 percent state, and 7.65 percent Social Security). $190 × .4365 = $83; $190 – $83 = $107. This would have made her plan cheaper than Michael's.

ALLISON'S FRINGE BENEFITS ($)

	Stay-at-Home Cost		Cost with Second-Income Fringe Benefit*		Cost or Value of Benefit**		Monthly Perk (+) or JRE (–)
1. Health insurance	125	–	190	=	0†	=	0
2. Retirement plan	0	–	96	=	–96	=	–96 JRE
3. Airline tickets	700	–	1,600	=	–900 ÷ 12 months	=	–75 JRE
4. Disability insurance	0	–	20	=	–20	=	–20 JRE
5. Life insurance	15	–	0	=	15	=	15 perk
6. Company car	1,833	–	800	=	1,033 ÷ 12 months	=	86 perk
7. Football tickets	180	–	780	=	–600 ÷ 12 months	=	–50 JRE
8. Country-club membership	0	–	1,800	=	–1,800 ÷ 12 months	=	–150 JRE
9. Expense account	0	–	0	=	0	=	0
Total monthly value or cost of fringe benefit package							–$290 JRE

NOTE: If you have a child-care account through a cafeteria plan, don't list it here. Child-care cost should have been listed in chapter one and tax savings from the plan included in chapters 7, 8, and 9. If you're trying to eyeball the value of a future cafeteria child-care benefit, see how to figure its value in chapter 7's postscript #2 and subtract value from taxes owed in chapters 7, 8, and 9.

* Tax influence is included in cost of each benefit to show Allison's fringe package's real worth. If deductible and taxable benefits were included on your federal and state tax returns, their effects are included (and hidden) in chapters 7, 8, and 9 and should not be computed into costs here. If, however, you are evaluating the value of a future benefit, include tax influence, if any, in benefit's worth.

** If benefit's value is an annual number, divide by 12 (months) to determine monthly perk (+) or JRE (–).

† ENTER 0 when results are negative. It's assumed that you will enroll in the cheaper health plan or that the increased benefits under the more expensive plan will offset extra cost.

2. *Retirement Plan:* Allison paid nothing into a retirement plan before working at the airline (column 1) and $150 per month after (column 2). The following tax note applies to her column 2 figure.

TAX NOTE: Her 401(k) retirement contribution was subtracted from her wages on her W–2 Wage and Tax Statement, box 1, but not from her Social Security and Medicare wages, boxes 3 and 5. Therefore, she saved paying income tax, but did not save paying Social Security and Medicare tax, on the $150. Because her income fell in the 28 percent federal bracket and 8 percent state bracket, Allison saved about 36 percent of her monthly contribution ($150 × .36 = $54) in income tax. Her after-tax cost was thus $96 ($150 –$54).

3. *Free Airline Tickets:* The airline gave employees and their immediate families free standby airline tickets. Before Allison began working for the airline she spent $700 per year (column 1) on tickets to visit her parents twice a year. After she began working, these tickets were free, but she and her husband couldn't resist an extra vacation and spent a week in Florida the first winter. Although all plane tickets were free, their Florida lodging, meals, and entertainment cost $1600 (column 2). (The next year it was Colorado, the next, Hawaii. . . .) The vacation temptation helped put their financial goal on "standby."

TAX NOTE: Sometimes free or discounted merchandise is taxable, but Allison's tickets met current nontaxable guidelines.

4. *Disability Insurance:* Allison paid nothing (column 1) for long-term disability insurance before she began

Some job benefits which end up JREs could be listed under different chapters. For example, clothing bought with an employee discount could be classified personal upkeep (chapter 2); the cost of Allison's Florida vacation could go under rewards (chapter 6). If JREs can be classified in more than one way, be sure you include them in only *one* chapter. Allison may decide later to move the Florida vacation to rewards (chapter 6), but the final result for spendable income will remain the same.

Occasionally, a fringe benefit may also be one of your financial goals, listed in the introduction, page 14. If Allison's Florida vacation were one of her goals, she should not include its cost in this chapter. Note, however, that listing a goal doesn't mean it's affordable. Allison's spendable income may be so disappointing that she must reconsider the need for an extra vacation every year.

working. After, however, she decided to insure a part of her salary. She paid $20 per month for a policy that would have cost much more if she hadn't purchased it through the airline. Still, her benefit cost $20 per month (column 2).

TAX NOTE: No tax effect here. The cost was not deductible or taxable.

5. *Life Insurance:* Allison spent $15 per month (column 1) on life insurance before she began working for the airline. The airline provided a policy for the same coverage at no cost (column 2), netting Allison a perk of $15 when she dropped her old policy.

Tax Note: Allison's life insurance benefit was not taxable. Employer-paid insurance premiums are not taxable on policies worth less than $50,000.

6. *Company Car:* Allison was provided a company car and permitted to drive it for personal use, which saved her and Michael the expense of owning a second car. They estimated a (not-as-nice) second car would have cost them about $1,833 per year (the same amount the airline valued Allison's personal use of the car), column 1.

Tax Note: Personal use of an employer-provided car is a taxable fringe benefit. So the $1,833 was added to Allison's income (*and* her Social Security and Medicare income) on her W–2. Thus the $1,833 was subject to income tax *and* Social Security and Medicare taxes. With tax brackets totaling 43.65 percent (28 percent federal, 8 state and 7.65 Social Security), Allison paid an extra $800 (column 2, $1,833 × .4365) in taxes for her car benefit.

7. *Football Tickets:* The airline gave free season football tickets to junior and senior executives. Allison disliked sports, but Michael was determined not to waste her wonderful fringe benefit. So they attended every game! Allison privately figured if she hadn't been so fortunate, they would have attended two games at a cost of $120 for four (not-as-good) tickets plus $30 per game for parking, programs, and food (column 1).

Instead, however, they attended ten games with no ticket cost but the same $30-per-game expense for parking, programs, and food ($30 × 10 = $300). That wasn't the end of Allison's expense for the tickets though.

Tax Note: Occasional tickets to sporting events given by an employer are usually nontaxable. Season tickets, however, hardly meet the IRS's definition of *occasional.* The two season tickets were valued at $1,100 and included in Allison's taxable income. Because her income tax and Social Security rates totaled 43.65 percent, she paid an extra $480 ($1,100 × .4365) in taxes because of the tickets. Cost for the ten games thus totaled $780 ($300 + $480) and is listed in column 2.

8. *Country-Club Membership:* Free country-club membership was another financial drain. Allison would rather have gone fishing, but she realized participation in country-club life was a rung on the corporate ladder. So she spent $840 on golf clubs and lessons even though she hated golf. There was more to her cost though.

TAX NOTE: The $2,200 membership was a taxable benefit. With Allison's income tax and Social Security rates totaling 43.65 percent, the membership added an additional $960 ($2,200 × .4365) to her costs in column 2 ($840 + $960 = $1,800).

9. *Expense Account:* Allison had an expense account, which covered all her business costs, including hotels, meals, and entertainment while traveling. Because she was honest about her expenses, the expense account didn't alter her spendable income.

TAX NOTE: An expense account that covers only actual expense is usually not taxable, nor are the expenses deductible by the employee.

Seeing the aftermath of her benefit package helped Allison understand why her savings account remained stagnant; she tried to change spending patterns so that her income would have a more positive conclusion. Still, next year she may spend just as much money on golf, football games, and another vacation, so she needs to check these numbers annually.

PERKS *CAN* MAKE A DIFFERENCE

After watching Allison's perks turn to dust, you may be feeling hopeless about the value of your fringe benefit package. Let's return to a more encouraging example: the waitress in the introduction. Her fringe benefits seemed meager compared to Allison's, yet they contributed $150 per month to her spendable income (see the table on the next page).

1. *Health Insurance:* Family coverage cost $200 per month through her husband's employer. The restaurant paid all but $90 per month for an identical family plan.
2. *Free Coffee and Lunches:* The waitress worked an average of twenty days per month and would have spent about $1 per day on coffee and lunches (column 1) at home. Coffee and lunches were free for restaurant employees, and the benefit was nontaxable (column 2).
3. *Leftovers:* The restaurant also allowed employees to take surplus food home occasionally. This amounted to a small nontaxable benefit of about $20 per month.

The same fringe benefit can have different values, depending on your tax bracket, needs, and financial goals. A flashy list of benefits, such as Allison's, can have disappointing effects on spendable income; a short list, such as the waitress's, can contribute significantly to spendable income.

THE WAITRESS'S FRINGE BENEFITS ($)

	Stay-at-Home Cost		Monthly Cost with Second-Income Fringe Benefit		Monthly Perk (+) or JRE (−)
1. Health insurance	200	−	90	=	110 perk
2. Lunches and coffee	20	−	0	=	20 perk
3. Leftovers	20	−	0	=	20 perk
Total monthly value or cost of fringe benefit package					$150 perk

ADD IT UP

A worksheet for figuring the value of your fringe benefits is on the following page. The results may surprise you.

YOUR FRINGE BENEFITS ($)

	Stay-at-Home Cost		Cost with Second-Income Fringe Benefit*		Cost or Value of Benefit**		Monthly Perk (+) or JRE (–)
1. Health insurance	_____	–	_____	=	_____†	=	_____
2. Retirement plan	_____	–	_____	=	_____	=	_____
3. Free or discounted merchandise	_____	–	_____	=	_____	=	_____
4. Other	_____	–	_____	=	_____	=	_____
5. Other	_____	–	_____	=	_____	=	_____
Total monthly value or cost of fringe benefit package							$_____‡

NOTE: If you have a child-care account through a cafeteria plan, don't list it here. Child-care cost should have been listed in chapter 1 and tax savings from the plan included in chapters 7, 8, and 9. If you're trying to eyeball the value of a future cafeteria child-care benefit, see how to figure its value in chapter 7's postscript #2 and subtract value from taxes owed in chapters 7, 8, and 9.

* If deductible and taxable benefits were included on your federal and state tax returns, their effects are included (and hidden) in chapters 7, 8, and 9 and should not be computed into costs here. If, however, you are evaluating the value of a future benefit, include tax influence, if any, in benefit's worth.

** If benefit's cost or value is an annual number, divide by 12 (months) to determine monthly perk (+) or JRE (–).

† ENTER 0 when results are negative. It's assumed that you will enroll in the cheaper health plan or that the increased benefits under the more expensive plan will offset extra cost.

‡ ENTER perk (+) as positive number or JRE (–) as negative number on the perks row on Your Second-Income JREs worksheet, pages 12–13.

12

AND WHAT ELSE?

AFTER READING THE preceding chapters, you may find it difficult to imagine that your second income could possibly be winnowed away even further. Yet there are hundreds of other subtractions, each as individual as we are as people. Most of the following "And What Elses" don't apply to very many of us, but if even one subtraction (or addition) fits your circumstance, it can make a difference. Some of those listed are so trivial it seems fussy to mention them, but they are explained to help you get started on your own And What Else numbers.

LOSS ON FIRST INCOME

Studies show that husbands in management positions whose wives stay home earn more than men whose wives work outside of the home. A study done at Pace University in New York found that men with MBAs who have stay-at-home wives earn 25 percent more than men who have wives who work outside of the home. Loyola University of Chicago research showed that fathers in management whose wives stayed home got raises 20 percent higher than men with employed wives. Reasons for the two-income penalty are difficult to identify. Working couples often have stalled incomes because they must tie their careers to the same geographic area. Which partner's career bites the bullet is a complicated decision. Yet with women still earning on average only 73 cents for every dollar men earn, most couples move with the husband's transfers and promotions.

But the supportive husband may also get passed up for a promotion if he can't stay late at the office because it's his turn to fix dinner or pick up the kids. Wives have always faced this handicap. Husbands do, too, when they (rightfully) assume more responsibility at home.

Working wives whose husbands opt to stay home should see a rise in income similar to that of the men in the above studies. There is bound to be a better chance for promotion when the first-income partner has more time and energy, because of fewer home responsibilities, to devote to his or her career.

If Brad had refused a transfer and promotion to benefit Sally's career, the after-tax value of his lost raise would have been a JRE on Sally's income. Likewise, if he had missed a raise because his extra efforts were spent on helping out at home rather than climbing the promotion ladder at work.

DONATIONS

Nonprofit charities will shiver here. Donations based on a percentage of income are JREs, because if you had no income, you'd make no donations. On the other hand, if you'd donate the same amount, no matter what your second income, then donations are not JREs. Let your conscience decide how much you donate, but also be aware of the effect donations have on an already precarious spendable income.

THE SANDWICH GENERATION

Couples are having children later than ever before and their parents are living longer. Sociologists like to refer to these couples, caught between responsibilities to their children and aging parents, as the "sandwich generation." The woman in the preface with three children and parents who also depended on her was a part of this phenomenon.

Obligations to aging parents often involve spending time, money, or both. But, as explained earlier, *time is money!* If you spend the time to help, you may not have the time to earn extra income; if you spend the time to earn, you may not have the time to help. By working, the woman in the preface may have faced more financial responsibility to her parents because, without the time to help, she needed to pay others to relieve her responsibilities. That cost is a job-related expense if she would have spent time helping if she didn't have a time shortage because of her job.

Of course, aging parents often pay for services themselves. Sally's parents lived only ten minutes away. Although they were unable to do many things for themselves, they were financially able to pay for help. They paid an average of $12 per hour for household help, meal preparation, yard care, and chauffeur, delivery services, and used eight hours of help each week (8 hours × $12 × 4.3 weeks per month = $413 per month). The only thing they couldn't buy was *time* with their grandchildren. And visits were growing further and further apart after Sally began working.

Brad and Sally overlooked what might have been a perfect solution to their financial dilemma. Although they were determined not to accept financial help from her parents, they could have helped each other, and all three generations would have benefited. Sally could have spent two mornings a week helping her parents. They would have loved the extra time with her and the grandchildren. And instead of paying Sally for the time, they could have *given* her a $413 per month *tax-free* gift. (You can give up to $10,000 a year as a tax-free gift to each of as many people as you want. A husband and wife can give up to $20,000 to the same individual.) The money would have kept Brad and Sally's budget in the black and possibly saved their marriage.

How far the generations are willing to go with this depends on compatibility and willingness and ability of the older generation to contribute financially. Aging parents determined to stay in their own homes must realize that their children's *time is money* and see the bargain in giving to their children, rather than paying strangers.

Watch out, though. If the money parents give an adult child is *directly* related to the services provided by the child, the IRS may say the money is compensation for services (i.e., taxable income to the child), and not a true gift. A time-clock arrangement won't pass the IRS's definition of "gift." But who's to say if you want to help your folks with the yard work for no pay. And who's to say if they want to give you an annual cash gift. Just be sure the two happenings are not connected.

A STITCH IN TIME

"A stitch in time saves nine." Two-incomers often lack the time to apply this old saying to their home budgets. As a result, charities depend on good used clothing that donors never got around to repairing, many articles lacking no more than a button or simple seam repair.

"A stitch in time" applies to much more than clothing, though. Consider the unfixed storm-door latch which results in the wind bending the door beyond repair; the carpet stain, untreated until permanently set; the unsprayed shrubs destroyed by insects; the ruined tires, never taken for alignment; the split chair leg, neglected until beyond repair. . . .

You'll never have much if you don't take care of what you've got! If your second income creates a time crunch that results in losses that could have been prevented—their replacement costs are JREs. If you don't fix the dry rot around the window because you just can't get around to it, the $500 cost of replacing the entire window is a JRE.

LONG-DISTANCE PHONE CALLS

The busier you are, the more likely you are to put off letter writing in favor of a quick phone call. Keeping in touch with long-distance friends and relatives can thus be an expensive undertaking, depending on how many people you need to "reach out and touch."

Extra long-distance bills can mount up to a very large job-caused expense if you opt for calling, rather than writing, because of a time shortage. Or the extra cost can be nil, if you'd rather eat worms than write a letter, regardless of your time supply. A quick glance at recent phone bills will give you a fairly accurate idea on how much to count this JRE.

HOME LIBRARY COST

Only bookworms need consider this expense. I have a friend who somehow finds time to read a half dozen or so books per month in spite of a full-time career and family. She's Book-of-the-Month's best customer because, she says, she doesn't have time to drive to and from the public library, whose hours aren't convenient with her schedule. The walls of her home are lined with read-only-once books. An investment . . . maybe. More likely, a JRE, only a fraction of which will be recouped when she sells off the novels for fifty cents apiece at her next garage sale.

STRESS

When stress is job-related, its cost is a JRE. Some of us cope with stress by slowly exhaling deep breaths of air or taking quiet walks (these are still free). Others rely on tranquilizers, massages, exercise classes, yoga, facials, stress workshops, psychiatrists, cigarettes, drugs, alcohol, get-away-from-it-all vacations, and *food*.

If food is your tranquilizer of choice, your job-stress expense includes not only the extra food you eat, but also the money you spend to lose the resulting extra pounds. Ballet dancers and fashion models may have already listed weight-control costs under personal upkeep (chapter 2), because thin figures are necessary for them to keep or advance in their careers. Your boss probably doesn't care about your weight as long as you can get through the door.

If you planned to enroll in a step class, yoga seminar, or stress workshop whether or not you work, the cost isn't a JRE. But if you're spending money specifically to relieve office stress, it is. Likewise, any money you spend to break a bad habit you've taken up to relieve job stress—e.g., stop-smoking classes, or nicotine patches to give up your cigarette habit—is a JRE.

Remember, when stress is directly related to your work, its expense becomes a JRE. That cost can range between a fifty-cent can of pop and $150-per-hour for a psychiatrist.

"SEDUCTION" IN THE WORKPLACE (AND WEIGHT CONTROL)

Working at Dunkin' Donuts or Baskin-Robbins can be an "enlarging experience." Some workplaces are filled with caloric seducers that fatten employees at unbelievable rates. One McDonald's employee even claimed that his expanding waistline was caused by the greasy air absorbed through his skin.

Food seducers don't limit themselves to employees in restaurants and fast-food spots, though. A schoolteacher can gain weight on the starchy kid-pleasing meals served in the school cafeteria; an executive on business lunches; a factory worker on doughnut-filled coffee breaks; an office worker on the ceaseless supply of brownies, cakes, and cookies in the employee lounge brought by coworkers.

When the cost of removing these temptations from your hips isn't related to stress (see above) or personal upkeep (chapter 2), you can say you were seduced at work and list their cost here. (Of course, the calories will call your name, whether you're working at Baskin-Robbins or staying too near your own refrigerator. At home, though, the calories don't come in thirty-one flavors.)

UTILITIES

If you have the time to spend at it, it's possible to save money on utilities. Go to extremes, though, and you can end up living pioneer-style. Exercise care when appraising the value of meter watching and assessing the cost of utility JREs on a second income.

The following formula is used to find the operating cost of electric appliances:

$$\frac{\text{WATTS}^{\star} \times \text{RATE (per KWH)} \times \text{HOURS}}{1{,}000}$$

A dedicated light-bulb guard must catch and lecture one hundred people who each forget to turn off lights for one hour to save 48 cents a day, or $14.40 a month. For the light-bulb guard this translates, using the national average of 8 cents per kilowatt-hour and the assumption he or she is catching people using 60-watt bulbs, as follows:

$$\frac{60\text{ (watts)} \times .08\text{ (rate per KWH)} \times 100\text{ (hours)}}{1{,}000} = 48\text{ cents per day}$$

Of course, higher-wattage appliances use electricity at a faster rate. A 5,000-watt clothes dryer costs 40 cents an hour to operate:

$$\frac{5{,}000\text{ (watts)} \times .08\text{ (rate per KWH)} \times 1\text{ (hour)}}{1{,}000} = 40\text{ cents per hour}$$

Accordingly, staying at home can sometimes save on utilities. If it takes ten extra minutes to hang and take down clothes that would have taken an hour to dry in an electric dryer, you can save 40 cents for ten minutes' work, which translates to $2.40 per hour. Still, a slow way to save—but more remunerative than light-bulb guarding. You can further cut corners, for instance, by

⋆ If appliance lists amps rather than watts, find wattage by multiplying amps times voltage (usually 120 volts, except for 220 volt appliances like clothes dryers and ranges).

turning off the dishwasher after the wash cycle and letting the dishes air dry or by keeping coffee hot in a thermos rather than in an electric coffeemaker. There are all sorts of ways to scrimp on your utility bills. Much larger savings may be gained, though, by "keeping the home fires burning." It's possible to save on heating bills if you have a wood stove and you're home to keep it stoked. I did this while writing this book. The free firewood saved us several dollars a day as long as I stayed near the wood stove (and computer). Likewise, when the solar water system kicked in to its max in midafternoon, I was there to throw in a load of laundry and turn on the dishwasher before the water cooled down that night. The *hot* part of the water was thus free. When I left home for the day, the expensive propane furnace and water heater took over.

You can, however, go too far with comparing at-home and at-work utility costs. For example, if you rush off to work leaving five lights, a ceiling fan, and the bedroom radio on, what does it cost? If wattages total 350, figure as follows, allowing ten hours before you get home again:

$$\frac{350 \text{ (watts)} \times .08 \text{ (rate per KWH)} \times 10 \text{ (hours)}}{1000} = 28 \text{ cents per day}$$

Counting utility JREs like the above is hardly worth the effort, especially when you consider that you'd probably be using the same lights, fan, and radio if you were home all day.

It's also worth noting that there are utility dollars to be saved through working outside the home. You can, on average, save about 3 percent of your total heating (or cooling) bill for every degree you turn down the thermostat in the winter (or up, in the summer). Adjusting the thermostat before leaving for work may save on utilities and result in an *addition* to spendable income.

You'll have to examine your lifestyle to determine how much you save or spend staying home versus working to arrive at an accurate utility JRE. Unless you have a wood stove to keep stoked, the dollar differences between at-home and at-work costs probably won't amount to much.

EARNED INCOME CREDIT

Low-income workers may be eligible to receive a bonus on their tax returns known as the earned income credit (EIC), Form 1040, line 56a (or Form 1040A, line 29c; or Form 1040EZ, line 8). In 1997 the credit was worth as much as $3,656 for workers with more than one qualifying child and earned income below $29,290; $2,210 for workers with one qualifying child and income below $25,760; and $332 for workers with no qualifying children and income below $9,770. The credit is refundable even if you owe no tax. Usually tax credits are used to reduce tax owed, but if the EIC exceeds tax liability you get the excess back in *cash*.

The credit is meant to give low-income workers an incentive to stay off welfare rolls and to offset their tax load. It has an unplanned result, though, for low-income two-paycheck families. A second income can push family income above the specified limit, therefore causing loss of the EIC. The lost credit due to a second income is thus a JRE for second incomers whose family income would otherwise have qualified for the EIC. Check Form 1040, 1040A, or 1040EZ instructions to see how much your EIC would be without your second income. Any lost credit is a JRE.

MONEY-SAVING HOBBIES

A second income's usefulness can be reduced if it leaves you no time to pursue a money-saving hobby such as sewing, cooking, gardening, woodworking, garage saling, landscaping, decorating/remodeling, making homemade gifts. . . . Most hobbies, of course, have little potential for saving money and even greater potential for spending it. Many fishermen try to convince themselves and their families that they are saving on the grocery bill. Birdwatchers and mountain climbers have even tougher arguments to muster.

Without a doubt, what to some of us are hobbies are to others tedious chores.

> So long as a man rides his hobbyhorse peaceably and quietly along the King's highway, and neither compels you or me to get up behind him,—pray, Sir, what have either you or I to do with it?
>
> —Laurence Sterne (c. 1760), *Tristram Shandy*

It's tempting to justify the cost and time we spend on hobbies with inflated projections of dollar savings. Gardening articles make exaggerated claims on how a

The IRS says *income* from hobbies is taxable. So, any hobby income should have been included under federal income tax (chapter 7).

But money *saved* from hobbies is invisible to Uncle Sam's eyes and is yours to keep. Remember, a penny saved is often worth two earned.

small plot of ground can save hundreds of dollars. Yet, you probably spend less than $2 per day ($730 per year) on your family's total vegetable intake. Subtract fertilizer, bug spray, seed, water, equipment, and the cost of those vegetables that won't do well in your growing zone, and you may find gardening a poor money saver. On the other hand, there's the ever-proliferating zucchini plant. You can grow a bumper crop on a tiny plot, feed your family for a year (if they'll stand for it), and still have zucchini to use in gift breads and muffins.

Gourmet cooking is an expensive hobby requiring unusual and expensive ingredients. The cook, however, who enjoys concocting one hundred ways to prepare ground beef may save money on the food budget. Home decorating, remodeling, and antique restoration can be expensive hobbies. But if the job has to be done, one way or the other, and budget decorating or furniture refinishing is your expertise, the money you could have saved (with the time your second income consumed) is a JRE.

Don't list savings you've already included in other chapters. A home seamstress could include lost savings to ready-made clothes under timesavers (chapter 4), and the coupon clipper could record lost savings under rushed shopping (chapter 5).

Evaluate the money-saving capacity of your hobby carefully. When time spent earning a second income interferes with your hobby's money-saving potential, the lost savings is a JRE.

THE TIN CUP

In most large offices, people are constantly getting married, having babies, retiring, or dying—inevitably followed by someone with a tin cup collecting for gifts or flowers. Each worker may also be expected to contribute to United Way and other charities—plus gourmet pastries in the staff lounge. All this, compounded by coworkers selling candy for their kids' soccer teams, Christmas cards to save the whales, and beef jerky for Seeing Eye dogs. Some days it might be cheaper to take an unpaid leave. These expenses are all JREs.

INSURANCE COLLECTING

Insurance companies have a special, underhanded way to increase profits—they deny legitimate claims submitted by policyholders. Millions of Americans have found that collecting what's rightfully theirs from tightfisted insurance companies is a time-consuming, bureaucratic nightmare. The maze of forms, phone calls, and letters it takes to fight a denial proves to be too frustrating and time-consuming for many policyholders, and they just

BIZARRO By DAN PIRARO

Dan Piraro's "Bizarro" cartoon is reprinted by permission of Chronicle Features, San Francisco, California.

give up and pay the disqualified bill themselves. That's just what the insurance industry banks on.

With the *time* to keep meticulous records and haggle with letters and phone calls, you can beat them down. Out-badgering an insurance company yourself can be one of life's most satisfying achievements.

Without the time to contest unjust denials, many two-income families pay claims out of their own pockets. This cost is a JRE for the second incomer who would gladly have taken up the challenge, except for a lack of time.

GUARANTEE FOLLOW-UP

Many products are marketed with unconditional, double-your-money-back, or satisfaction-guaranteed promises. One reason for Sam Walton's exceptional success with Wal-Mart was his the-customer-is-always-right approach.

Nevertheless, watch for guarantees that are designed to inspire your confidence in the product and yet depend on your apathy not to demand compensation. Several years ago Sears guaranteed the knees in one line of jeans to outlast the jeans. Any parent knows kids will rate spinach over candy before seats outlast knees in their pants.

The Sears guarantee was a red flag to buyers with the time to play the game. Yet Sears was secure from a major loss because customers had to present original sales receipts with claims, and they had to take restitution in new jeans—*the same size.* By taking time to follow the rules of the game, one mother with a stair-step family saved hundreds of dollars.

A grocery store guaranteed double-your-money-back on items their new price scanners mispriced. What a joy this was to one shopper until the word spread and the store began checking their scanner entries. It had been so easy to "scan" the tape before leaving the store and ask for reimbursement. Yet most shoppers left too hurriedly and lost the price tape before returning the next week.

If a car doesn't live up to its 50,000-mile warranty, most owners are at the car dealer's door. But the makers of smaller items depend on few buyers taking the time to hunt them down and demand satisfaction. Cathy will find it quicker to buy a new coffeemaker

cathy® **by Cathy Guisewite**

IN 1970, WE FOUGHT EVERY INJUSTICE... TODAY, I DON'T HAVE TIME TO RETURN ONE DEFECTIVE APPLIANCE.
IN 1970, WE SHUT DOWN ENTIRE INSTITUTIONS TO MAKE OUR VOICES HEARD... TODAY, I DON'T HAVE TIME TO WRITE ONE LETTER OF COMPLAINT.
IN 1970, WE ORGANIZED A GENERATION TO REVOLUTIONIZE THE PRIORITIES AND POLITICS OF THE WHOLE SOCIAL STRUCTURE... TODAY, I DON'T HAVE THE ENERGY TO LOOK UP ONE PHONE NUMBER AND MENTION I'M DISSATISFIED.
REBEL WITHOUT A COFFEEMAKER.

than to return her old one. Guarantee follow-up takes time! Lost reimbursements are JREs to second incomers who would keep the business world honest, except for a time shortage.

HOME OFFICE EXPENSE

If you met IRS requirements to claim your home office as a deductible job expense, the cost should have been listed under deductible job expenses, chapter 10. But rules for claiming a home office as a tax deduction are especially arduous; employees seldom qualify for an office-in-home deduction. Among other rules, the office must be for the convenience of your employer—not just helpful to you. Check rules carefully before claiming a home office deduction.

Just because you can't meet IRS guidelines, though, doesn't mean you don't have office expenses. The cost of a desk, chair, bookshelves, filing cabinet, office supplies, reference books, and utilities to heat and cool your office can all be JREs, even though they are not tax deductible.

You may have already listed the cost of nondeductible office timesavers such as a computer, software, fax and copy machines, and phone accessories under timesavers, chapter 4. If not, include their costs here also.

STUDENT AID

A frequent reason for adding a second income to a family's resources is to pay for college expenses. Yet the extra income can be self-defeating. Many scholarships, grants, loans, and student work programs are based on need, and a second income may push your family out of the "needy" bracket. Student aid lost due to a second income is a JRE. However, it's difficult to gauge what might and might not have been. You shouldn't count this hard-to-verify loss as a job expense unless you know for a fact that your child was disqualified from receiving financial aid because of your second income. Income and grade requirements are usually not spelled out well enough so that student aid lost by a second income can be reliably identified.

PENNY PINCHING

With the time, you can pinch pennies until they scream. What sickens your best friend may delight you; what you think of as moneygrubbing, she calls thrifty. Don't let someone else's concept of "cheapness" deter you from penny pinching to your heart's delight.

The possibilities for pinching are endless. You can use cloth napkins versus paper, mow with a push mower, recycle vacuum cleaner bags, collect aluminum cans, as well as make homemade bread, greeting cards, and wrapping paper. The vision of a thrifty sister-in-law collecting beer cans and meeting a snake face to face at the bottom of a park trash barrel illustrates too well why many frugal souls give up the quest. Choose "pinchers" that won't make life so uncomfortable that you can't stick with them.

Penny pinching is cumulative, so even though one pinch doesn't save much, the net result of a good list of penny-pinching habits can be fruitful. If time shortage due to a second income keeps you from penny pinching, the lost savings are a second-income JRE.

If you want to pursue skinflinting to the max, read *The Tightwad Gazette, The Tightwad Gazette II,* and *The Tightwad Gazette III,* by Amy Dacyczyn (Villard Books, 1993, 1995, 1996, $12.99 each). These books offer money-saving tips that might make even Ebenezer Scrooge blush, but they could inspire you to make a real difference in your bottom line.

OTHER . . .

And what else?? Think it over carefully. There may be several more listings you should include. Some may even have a positive effect on spendable income. If you drop Tuesday morning bowling, neighborhood chauffeuring, Cub Scout den mothering, and holiday hostessing duty when you return to work, the money saved is an *addition* to spendable income.

ADD IT UP

Sally and Brad got too busy to write to Brad's parents, who lived three hundred miles away. Instead, they called

SALLY'S AND WHAT ELSE? EXPENSE ($)

Loss on first income	
Donations	
Sandwich generation	
A stitch in time	
Long-distance phone calls	−25
Home library cost	
Stress	
"Seduction" (and weight control)	−32
Utilities	
Earned income credit	
Money-saving hobbies	
The tin cup	
Insurance collecting	
Guarantee follow-up	
Home office expense	
Student aid	
Penny pinching	
Other	+10
Other	
Other	
Other	
Other	
Other	
Total And What Else JRE (−) or Perk (+)	−$47 JRE

NOTE: Do not include expenses listed in previous chapters. Divide annual costs by 12 (months).

YOUR AND WHAT ELSE? EXPENSE ($)

Loss on first income	______
Donations	______
Sandwich generation	______
A stitch in time	______
Long-distance phone calls	______
Home library cost	______
Stress	______
"Seduction" (and weight control)	______
Utilities	______
Earned income credit	______
Money-saving hobbies	______
The tin cup	______
Insurance collecting	______
Guarantee follow-up	______
Home office expense	______
Student aid	______
Penny pinching	______
Other	______
Other	______
Other	______
Other	______
Total And What Else JRE (–) or Perk (+)	$______ ⋆

NOTE: Do not include expenses listed in previous chapters. Divide annual costs by 12 (months).
⋆ ENTER JRE (–) as negative or perk (+) as positive number on the And What Else row on Your Second-Income JREs worksheet, pages 12–13.

his parents several times a month and noticed a $25 jump in their phone bill. Sally's doughnut-coffee breaks, fast-food lunches, and hours spent sitting at her desk caused her to gain fifteen pounds her first year at work. So she spent an extra $384 ($32 per month) on a treadmill so she could run off the extra weight. She *saved* $10 a month on a monthly luncheon which she no longer attended (see Sally's worksheet, page 182). Fill out Your And What Else? Expense numbers on page 183.

THE SEARCH IS OVER

Your list of JREs is finished! I hope you were able to keep close track, chapter by chapter, of where your income was headed. Recheck your math on Your Second-Income JREs worksheet, pages 12–13. Then, before you make a rash decision, read The Bottom Line, chapter 13.

13

The Bottom Line

THE BOTTOM LINE—or spendable income—is the main yardstick for those who work for dollars. It's what's left of a paycheck after factoring in all job-related expenses and perks. It's often the first (but usually not the only) reason for most double shifts.

Because job expenses wear so many disguises, many second incomers' incidental vocation is "money laundering." Money pours into their budgets, spins and agitates, and then pours down the JRE drain. As a result, the true financial benefit of some paychecks is so meager they don't contribute toward *any* financial aim. If Brad and Sally had tracked Sally's job expenses, they would have discovered her paycheck was an economic burden. Sally's effort to help out with the money problem was in vain, especially since she would rather have stayed home with their children.

Yet if you're not scrupulously honest about your numbers, this book can become the devil's playground for rationalizers and Peg Bundys (from TV's *Married with Children*). Keep in mind the old saying, "Figures never lie—but liars sometime figure." Insofar as you've been accurate and honest with JRE numbers, the bottom line on Your Second-Income JREs worksheet, pages 12–13, reveals the straight truth about your paycheck's financial strength. Unfortunately, though, there are no guidelines to evaluate the credibility of bottom-line numbers. Spendable incomes, all figured with legitimate numbers, can reveal terrifying holes in the dike or substantial—and unsuspected—benefits.

To be sure, a paycheck's spending capacity may be but one of many considerations. Your motives for working might include self-esteem, social respect, the desire to make a difference, or realize a dream, and happiness. Most often money is the main point of double shifts, but these other reasons may complicate judgments. The point is that once you've identified *all* your incentives for working and determined the true financial contributions of your income, you can make career decisions much more easily.

BOTTOM LINES CAN CHANGE

Because bottom-line numbers are likely to change, you should refigure them at least once a year. Even if your salary and benefits haven't changed, you can have large discrepancies in useful income from one year to the next. Thus, decisions based on bottom-line numbers aren't valid for a lifetime. Fortunately, only a limited number of fast-moving professions have career trains that leave the station just once.

Don't like what you see? There are five ways to increase your bottom-line numbers when spendable income is disappointing or inadequate:

1. Earn more money.
2. Reduce your JREs.
3. Change your financial goals.
4. Change careers or work part-time.
5. Quit work.

1. *Earn more money.* You can try working harder or longer hours in your present job (not a popular choice) or getting a higher-paying job in your line of work (well, *that* sounds easy).

2. *Reduce your JREs.* You can stay in your present job but reduce your JREs to increase the value of your income. Some JREs can be reduced once you recognize their effects. This, unfortunately, is not always a painless solution.

Tax JREs are not negotiable unless you're willing to risk spending time at the "big house." Most other JREs have room for compromise. The come-to-the-home nanny may have to go in favor of a less expensive day-care center. Maybe such an extravagant work wardrobe isn't all that necessary. Perhaps you can save by joining a car pool and cutting down on those lavish lunches. Instead of eating out so often at night, maybe you can organize a major cook-and-freeze project on the weekend. Or, you can stock up on healthy sandwich makings and other snacks and designate fix-your-own night(s).

Fire the housecleaner, learn to live with a little dust, and delegate cleaning responsibilities to your kids and your spouse. (After living with a husband and three sons who wouldn't recognize a dust bunny if it bit their big toes off, I recommend this idea with high hopes but also with reservation.) Look for your kid's abilities and genetic limitations. Maybe someone in your family really is dust-bunny-blind. But they're able to mow the yard, cook dinner, wash the car, do the laundry. . . .

Think about cheap ways to reward your family for all the things they give up because you work. Instead of an expensive computer game, introduce them to old-fashioned checkers—and play with them, and read to them or with them. Instead of sending the kids to that expensive summer camp, go on a family weekend camping trip. This gets tricky, though. Reward-guilt buys are often intended to replace the time you don't have to give. The time spent playing checkers or camping can cause an even bigger time shortage and thus a new spending cycle. So learn to just say No. Kids and payday are like sharks and blood. The kids smell the money and move in for the kill. (They say sharks can be fended off with a sharp blow to the nose.) Consider discussing with your kids why your job is important for you and for the family, instead of apologizing—in purchases—for why you're not always home. This may make it easier to scale down on reward-guilt buys.

If you have teenage children, keep a small sum of money in assorted denominations at home. Then delegate shopping errands (always providing the exact dollar amount—otherwise they'll expect tips). Having kids pick up the dry cleaning, a gallon of milk, the medical prescription . . . can save you hours a week and give you more time for the important shopping, as well as more time with your family.

You'll probably find other ways to cut back when you check your own expenses. Each JRE reduction may not amount to much, but when added together, they can make a sizable difference in what's left of your paycheck.

JREs also may change of their own accord. As children grow older, child-care (chapter 1) and timesaver expense (chapter 4) may drop. Not all changes are reductions, though. For example, a rise in first income can push the second income into a higher tax bracket (chapters 7 and 8).

3. *Change your financial goals.* After identifying the spending limits of your second income, reexamine your financial goals. It might be a miserable but smart economic decision to lower your expectations—at least for the time being. You may have to settle for a used, rather than a new car. The Disney World vacation may have to be replaced with a trip closer to home. The kids may have to work part-time to get through college. It's easy to assume, for instance, that an extra $500 payment can be absorbed when adding a second income to a family's budget. In Best Cases (Second-Income JRE Chart, pages 10–11), it will be. In Typical Cases, the extra payment is a money time bomb.

Even when a sorry bottom line is not the issue, you'll notice changes in your financial goals through the years.

Saving for the children's education won't always be a goal. Perhaps, though, you'll have long ago added a retirement plan to your goal list—and be able to afford it.

4. *Change careers or work part-time.* If you're netting less money than you need or tired of juggling your job and home responsibilities, perhaps you should consider a part-time job, or a complete career change. Anna Quindlen, Pulitzer Prize–winning columnist, changed careers recently. Even though her newspaper career was set on a rising star, she decided to stay home with her kids and write novels. Her career switch wasn't linked entirely to money, although she admitted money was a definite factor in her decision. Yet she was confident she could make an adequate living writing novels. A possible drop in income didn't cause her to forego her choice of writing at home and living at a slower pace. She said, "The only thing that can stop me from doing this is if I take other people's sense of what I ought to do and want as my own." There's no law that says you can't jump the track and change careers.

Sometimes, a different job, even lower paying or with fewer hours, may net a better bottom line. Deductible job expenses (chapter 10), personal upkeep (chapter 2), and transportation and lunches (chapter 3) can differ a lot between jobs. Moreover, part-time versus full-time work can significantly change the amount you spend on child care (chapter 1). And with fewer work hours, you're less likely to need expensive timesavers (chapter 4) or to shop on the run (chapter 5). So a fun part-time job can sometimes net a higher spendable income than the stressful or boring full-time job. Or, the trade-off between hours worked and spendable income may be more equitable. This was certainly true in my case, when I worked three hours a day for Senior Services.

A pressure-cooked teacher may enjoy teaching evening adult-education classes part-time, and clear more money than teaching high-school students carrying switchblades. A bored data processor may achieve a better bottom line working part-time at the painting she's always dreamed of doing. A young mother may clear just as much staying home with her child and babysitting that child's playmate. Don't discount the job you'd like; it may be a good economic choice.

5. *Quit work.* Take the plunge and quit your job—a radical step, yes; but if your paycheck is devoured by JREs it may be a good economic choice. However, if your paycheck still has some value after subtracting job expenses, no matter how small, be careful. Budgets hanging on the edge can be wrecked by the loss of even small sums. Clearly, you'll need to adjust your living standard if your second income has any post-JRE value. Financial benefits must be carefully weighed against the burden of producing the income.

Second incomers with strong money motives are most likely to quit work if they discover their incomes are being consumed by job expenses. Exercise extreme caution, however, before giving your two-week notice. It's true, budgets can be balanced by good money management. Unfortunately, though, some workers lack the self-discipline necessary to make homemaking a paying venture. Discuss this step with your partner.

Tackling tax laws, investments, interest rates, insurance terminology, guarantee litigation, and smart shopping techniques are often more challenging and stimulating than the work world. But only when pursued with wit, ambition, and creativity can homemaking be *financially* rewarding.

THE MONEY MOTIVE

Money is the inspiration and inducement keeping so many second incomers in the workforce. After decades of rhetoric, more and more women are now admitting that they continue their double shifts for their paychecks. A 1995 *Parents* magazine survey found only 4 percent of mothers, if given a choice without financial repercussions, want to work full-time. Superwomen are getting tired!

Nonetheless, career decisions, even for those with strictly money motives, can't usually be based solely on positive or negative numbers. Of course, second incomers with negative bottom lines (and only money motives) have easy decisions; their anthem is "Take This Job and

For Better or For Worse® **by Lynn Johnston**

Shove It." On the other hand, second incomers with substantial bottom lines (and only money motives) will feel financially bound to continue their double shifts. (Still, identifying spendable income is important to avoid the credit chaos that can result from overrating a paycheck's buying power.)

Decisions aren't so easy for those whose bottom-line numbers fall between the negative and substantial extremes. Most incomes have some financial merit, and you'll have to weigh time pressures against economic benefits. Ideally, the financial goals you can meet through a second income will be more important than the time your job demands. Because our goals and values vary, each earner's judgment is individual. Any two workers' decisions may be completely different depending on whether they're working for grocery money or for a vacation home. Of course, having money to feed the kids should take precedence over having time to take them to the zoo. However, a vacation condo purchased to ensure two weeks of quality time may not offset fifty weeks of "no zoos."

In most cases, workers must weigh more than money motives when they choose a career. You may *think* your paycheck is your only reason for working. But would you work the red-light district or sell drugs for a better income? If not, you have other factors to consider.

OTHER MOTIVES

Many laudable motives, other than money, justify second incomes. Even though dollars are important, to ignore these other incentives usually oversimplifies a complex decision. Some second incomers swear money is their only reason for working, but find that they also work for the satisfaction, the challenge. . . . Likewise, some second incomers say they work for the fulfillment, the prestige . . . but find their motives, in fact, intrinsically tied to the dollar bill. In addition, some work to avoid what's at home: housework, bake sales, hyperactive kids, volunteer work, taxi service, and marauding bands of visiting relatives and kaffeeklatsch neighbors.

There are jobs that are challenging, fulfilling—and even fun. They can be so satisfying that money becomes a side issue. Yet most jobs are called work because that's what they are, and few people will sign on to do them without a money payoff (unless there's a visit pending from Uncle Elmo and his twelve kids).

The contest is to find the job with the best combination of income, challenge, fulfillment . . . When the paycheck is too small, most workers seek satisfaction elsewhere, in their personal lives or another job (unless the phone rings, and it's Uncle Elmo).

cathy® **by Cathy Guisewite**

Yet money doesn't always enter into career decisions. When the lawyer in the introduction uncovered her income's true value, she wondered if her hectic schedule was justified. She loved her work, though, and her identity and self-image were closely linked to her job title and what *others* thought she earned. Weekends filled with preschool chatter and squabbles left her looking forward to Mondays. She also doubted the soundness of her marriage and felt a need to maintain a line to self-sufficiency. Even without a worthwhile money payoff, she stayed on the fast track. Career choices can't always be based on red and black numbers.

SELF-RESPECT, SOCIAL RESPECT, AND HAPPINESS

How good you feel about yourself (your self-respect, self-esteem, or whatever you want to name it), the social respect you are accorded by others, and your happiness are irreversibly mixed. For instance, to consider your happiness without taking into account your self-respect would result in a distorted evaluation of happiness. You aren't likely to count your life as happy if you consider yourself an underpaid drudge. You also aren't likely to be given much social respect if you have no self-respect. And around it goes. Self-respect, social respect, and happiness do not separate like oil and water in a clear measuring cup so that each can be measured separately.

Self-respect, if it could be judged alone, most often hinges on what *you* feel you are contributing to society. Are you doing something you think is worthwhile, through your job or volunteer work, at home, or all of the above? Are you challenged? Are you doing something important? If you are a parent, how well you feel you are rearing your children will influence your self-regard. You may feel the best example you can set for them is through your job, living the work ethic you hope to pass on. Or you may feel the better example would be a back-to-basics lifestyle, giving more of your time to your children and causes you believe in.

Social respect is most often gained through our jobs. In the last decades, society has come to undervalue "the hand that rocks the cradle." Any homemaker will tell you she dreads meeting new faces because of the inevitable Question: After exchanging names, it always comes—WHAT DO YOU DO? As soon as she acknowledges she is a homemaker, the social parry begins. Stereotypically perceived as a parasite on her husband's back, uninteresting, and not too intelligent or well-informed, she is either talked down to or cut from the conversation altogether. Defensive replies to the Question include saying she is a Cub Scout den mother, volunteer at the hospital, or chairman of the local United Way. This sort of answer is most often interpreted as "She can't get a paying job." Also, of course, a CEO with a large company is going to get more social respect than a worker on the assembly line when she answers the Question. You get the idea here.

It isn't fair or enlightened, but social respect or prestige these days generally hinges on what you do to earn a living. Many people will work for nothing rather than face the Question. As more men and women feel free to make the choice to stay at home, perhaps society will

learn to value people regardless of whether they draw a paycheck. Parents who stay at home deserve enormous respect for doing the toughest job in the world.

Happiness. Being happy is like being in love. When you're in love, you know it. When you're happy, you know it. There's no need to spend pages on this. Happy is happy. Would you be happier staying home, working part-time, or working full-time? Naturally, this depends on what's at home and what's at work. If your choices are a colicky baby and a toddler with the worst case of the terrible twos in pediatric history at home versus gutting chickens in a chicken-processing plant at work, "happy" isn't going to count for much here.

SPENDABLE INCOME VS. SATISFACTION LEVEL

Self-respect, social respect, and happiness blend together into what we'll call our satisfaction (or fulfillment) level, which for some workers is more important than spendable income. Spendable income is the only measure you need consider if your work motives are truly just dollars. Not many of us are as mercenary as we think, though. Even if you're sure money is your only job motive, take the time to check your satisfaction level. For those with exciting, challenging jobs (and well-to-do spouses), a high satisfaction level may be more important than spendable income. For everyone else, satisfaction level is still something to consider.

Politicians who spend millions of their own money to get elected to jobs that pay only thousands personify the importance of satisfaction levels. They live on independent income, perks they're not telling us about, some *very* high satisfaction levels, or all of the above.

Even though you're not an elected official, measuring your job's worth in dollar bills alone may result in a bad career decision. Granted, a job's worth is harder to evaluate when considering both satisfaction level and spendable income. Decisions get more complicated and aren't as clear-cut; spendable income can be identified almost to the last dollar; satisfaction level may be harder to gauge. The same job may rate entirely different satisfaction levels with different workers, or even with the same worker on good days and bad days. And which is more important, spendable income or satisfaction level? Their ratings depend a lot on your most recent work experiences and current financial condition.

To sort through the decision process, it may help to assign a point value to spendable income and satisfaction level.

Rank *spendable income* by what it contributes to your family's income:

Maximum 50 points:	*Can't live without it or it meets all financial goals, or both.
1–49 points:	Helps some; meets limited financial goals.
0 points:	Doesn't contribute at all.

Rank *satisfaction level* with a combination of your self-respect, social respect, and happiness ratings:

Maximum 50 points:	Love job; very satisfied; not missing any personal life.
1–49 points:	Like job; somewhat satisfied; missing some of personal life.
0 points:	Hate job; very unsatisfied; no time for personal life at all.

If Sally had read this book before the divorce, she would have assigned her at-work spendable income 0 points because it didn't contribute to family income. She liked her job somewhat but felt she was missing too much at home, so she would have given her at-work satisfaction level only 20 points. (Total at-work points, 20.)

* The above point system (100 points maximum) assumes you give equal importance to your spendable income and satisfaction level. Numbers can be adjusted according to your interests. If, for instance, spendable income is 80 percent of your decision and satisfaction level accounts for only 20 percent, you could assign 80, 1–79, and 0 points to spendable income; and 20, 1–19, and 0 to satisfaction level.

Her at-home scores: spendable income, 10 points, because she saved a little money by staying home; satisfaction level, 50 points, because she loved staying home with her kids and having time for other interests. She didn't worry about social respect. (Total at-home points, 60.)

SALLY'S AT-HOME AND AT-WORK SCORES

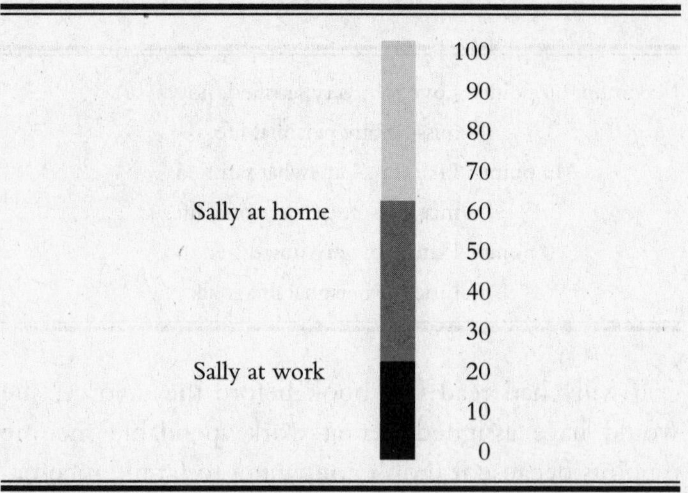

Julie, the part-time music teacher in chapters 4 and 7, had very few JREs and thus netted a high return on her $12,000 income. She ranked her at-work spendable income at 50 points because it met her reasonable list of financial objectives. She also loved her job, felt good about herself, and missed nothing at home, so she listed her at-work satisfaction level at 50 points. (Total at-work points, 100.)

Not working at all, Julie would have ranked her at-home spendable income at 0 points. When deciding on her at-home satisfaction level, she recognized that at-home and at-work satisfaction levels often interrelate. If she had stayed home, she would have been miserable, knowing she could and should be contributing financially to her family's income. She also believed she would have less social respect because she didn't "do anything." So she rated her at-home satisfaction level at only 20 points. (Total at-home points, 20.)

JULIE'S AT-HOME AND AT-WORK SCORES

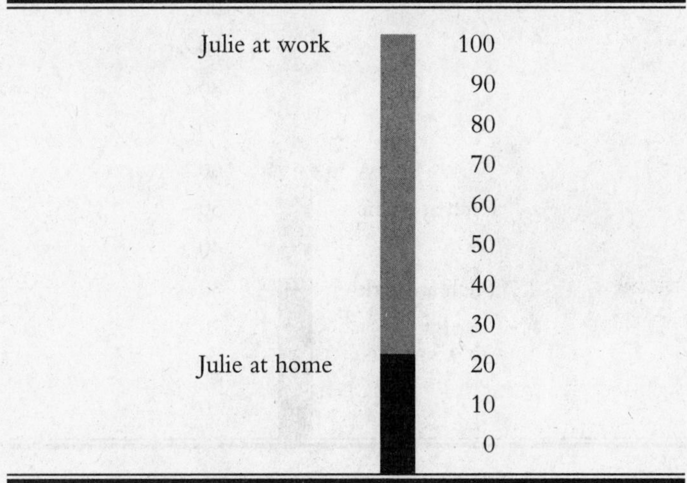

Rich, who took a leave of absence from his job to work at home on a better robot design (chapters 1, 4, 7, and 10), found he kept only about $16,000 of his

$60,000 income after job expenses were subtracted. He and his wife, Marcy, were surprised that the one-income life was so possible and decided that Marcy would take her turn at home after Rich finished his project. Rich and Marcy could see the financial result of losing their second income was not nearly as dire as they had expected—whether one of them lost his or her income due to layoff, illness, by choice to follow a dream, or to be a full-time parent.

RICH'S AT-HOME AND AT-WORK SCORES

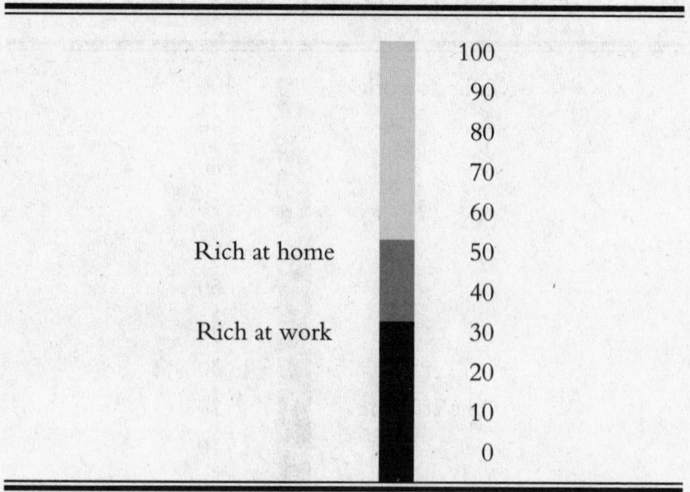

Rich could only give his at-work spendable income 20 points when he saw how little of it he actually kept. Because of office politics, the long commute to and from work, and the repetitiveness of his work, he only ranked his at-work satisfaction level 10 points. (Total at-work points, 30.)

At home, Rich had 0 points for spendable income (but he has visions of an income that will beat winning the lottery if his robot sensor ideas work); and 50 points, satisfaction level. (Total at-home points, 50.)

The higher the combined total of spendable income and satisfaction level, whether at-home or at-work, the better the option. Scores above 80 are almost always good choices, and scores below 20 cry out for other alternatives. Between 20 and 80 points is a gray stretch of numbers which may not lead to such quick answers. Two equal at-work scores of, say, 50 points do not necessarily result in the same decision. Giving spendable income 50 points, because your family can't make it without your income, and 0 points to satisfaction level, because you hate your job, leaves you working or looking for another job. If you score 50 points (25 points on spendable income, plus 25 points on satisfaction level), however, your decision is more difficult, depending greatly upon your at-home score and if you are able and willing to give up the limited financial goals your income makes possible.

The point system may help with career decisions if you like to fiddle with numbers and can be honest with their assigned values. Candid rating of your satisfaction level and spendable income is essential though. Remember, figures never lie, but liars sometime figure!

If choices based on numbers make you uncomfortable, don't be afraid to trust your heart and instincts. Good judgment and intuition may lead to decisions that are quicker and just as valid.

> The truth was felt by instinct here,
> —[a] Process which serves a world of trouble and time.
>
> —Robert Browning

THE PINK-COLLAR PREDICAMENT

Through the economic law of supply and demand, overcrowding in the job market has produced a class of pink-collar jobs—occupations not necessarily lacking in skill or education requirements, but low-paying and traditionally held by women. The pink-collar problem endures partly because of the glass ceiling, an invisible prejudice that keeps women from rising to higher-paying jobs. At the same time, women often cannot or do not aim for better job opportunities in order to keep up with their after-five shifts. In effect, they stand on a sticky floor while reaching for the glass ceiling. The glass ceiling has been blamed for women's scarcity in the higher echelons of the job world, but the sticky floor has an equal influence.

Labor economist Frank Levy says that if fewer women join the pink-collar workforce, their labor will be more scarce and not so undervalued. In other words, the fewer women who work, the higher wages will be for those who remain or return to the job market!

Thanks, but no thanks. Everyone wants a better income. It's impossible to imagine the have-nots stepping aside so that the haves can have more; the have-nots with the time to enjoy life and family but no income, and the haves with the income but no time.

cathy® **by Cathy Guisewite**

The pink-collar predicament could be resolved with shorter workweeks, telecommuting programs, and job-sharing, part-time, and flex-time plans. These options offer women a way to really have it all—career, income, and family life—without the fast track. In addition, with a smaller number of worker hours available, the pink-collar worker might not be so limited and underpriced.

Pay equity will become a reality only through the natural pressures of supply and demand. Activists would do well to concentrate on improving the lot of the part-time worker. In the past, the attitude of business toward job-sharing and part-time arrangements has been exploitative. Management has clung to the position that the more hours worked, the more serious and committed an employee is. With this false assumption, business has resisted giving part-time employees competitive wages and benefits prorated to hours worked. Yet, only with pay and benefit equity will part-time workers (mostly women) find a workable solution to their time and money conflicts.

Employers should recognize that part-time and job-sharing employees, if given fair wages and their share of fringe benefits, are often willing to work extra hours during emergencies or the annual rush season, thus saving the extra cost of hiring more employees or untrained temporary workers of doubtful value. Part-time and job-sharing employees can also cover for each other in case of sickness or family emergency and so are less likely to leave employers in the lurch. It should be whispered, so advantage isn't taken, but part-time employees may even be more likely than full-time employees to put in off-clock hours on a special report or project. This may be true because part-time and job-sharing workers are anxious to prove themselves, and they have more flexible schedules.

Employers should also consider the advantages of telecommuting programs. More than nine million Americans now work either part-time or full-time at home rather than going into the office. Businesses find telecommuters save them money on office space and that they accomplish more work without the distraction of coworkers. The workers save time by not commuting to work, by not having to spend time getting ready for work, and by using break and lunch periods to do household chores rather than drink coffee.

UNCLE SAM'S CROCODILE TEARS

For decades two-incomers have argued for help from Uncle Sam. And he feigns concern. That's it. He'll never do much more unless there's something in it for him. It's in his best interest to keep as many two-income couples working as he can because of his tax take on their incomes (see chapter 7). Still, as long as the job market is saturated, he has no reason to encourage *more* people to punch time clocks.

Free child care has been on wish lists for years. It won't happen; but even if it did, it would most likely only encourage more competition for jobs already in short supply. In time, free child care would only lower wages and do nothing for parents' time problems. Even Uncle Sam can see it isn't smart to provide too many incentives so that more people—particularly women—will try to move into an already crowded workforce.

VIEWPOINTS

If respect must be linked to money, it should not be further tied to the grading scale of A+ for money earned and D– for money saved. A+ grades rightfully belong to those who earn, *or save,* enough money to achieve a desired standard of living, and who also have the time to enjoy it. D– grades belong to those who don't even try to earn *or save* the money necessary for their families to live decently.

Cutting remarks separate the two sisterhoods, which should be reaching toward each other. "They just stay home and bake cookies" is the attitude full-time careerists often unwittingly reveal toward full-time homemakers. Full-time homemakers counter with remarks such as "They work to buy BMWs." To the sisters smart enough to outmaneuver the time clock, we should offer respect and congratulations. To those who choose careers—approval and best wishes. Except for the Peg

Bundys, most of us choose to do what is best emotionally and financially for ourselves and our families.

As I hope this book has demonstrated, second incomes don't always yield economic benefits. Bottom-line numbers will show the way for a few to return to the June Cleaver era, if they so desire. Full-time homemaking, with plenty of friends around employed in the same business, can produce some of the happiest years of your life. I recall with fondness those years when we mothers let our children play in the park while we solved world problems and played tennis, sat for each other's kids, were involved in community and school activities—and still had time to practice the money-management tactics discussed in this book. We, our families, schools, and communities were better for it—and the money-stretching strategies worked!

I thought about writing this book years ago when friends and neighbors, one by one, began to join the full-time clock race. They mostly did it for the money, and I wondered why they didn't see the part-time solution as I did. My family seemed as well off; but maybe I was wrong. Maybe I too would have to join the full-time parade if we were to get the boys through college, build our dream house, and retire before we were burned out and used up. I had to *live* the book before I wrote it.

Now, our three bottomless-pit sons are grown, educated, and gone—and not one of them thinks we didn't keep up with the Joneses. We've built our dream house. Jim's planning on retiring before age sixty. And, except for our first three years of marriage, I've never worked full-time.

CHOICES

The two-income myth has convinced almost two-thirds of America's married couples that when money matters, a second paycheck is the best solution. Yet the trade of time for money hasn't always been a bargain. Married women have entered the workforce, often without recognizing the limitations of their paychecks and time. Time has become a commodity, usually selling to the highest bidder. Unfortunately, the sales are final and can't be revoked.

I hope this book makes you aware of your options. Not all second incomes are as worthwhile as they appear. Those hoping, however, for quick solutions and summaries in these last pages will be disappointed. Chapter-by-chapter evaluation of your income is necessary to make financially sound decisions. Plus, careful examination of your other work motives is essential. There is no "best" move that is right for everyone. Financial benefit of a second income and motives for working must be carefully weighed against time supply. The scales will tip decisively for some, while others will find the choices not so clear-cut and agreeable. So, what's best for you and your family may be wrong for your best friend. Whatever your decision, though, remember:

> What you can do, or dream you can, begin it,
> Boldness has genius, power, and magic in it.
>
> —Goethe, *Faust*

INDEX

About the Author

LINDA KELLEY is a homemaker and first-time book author. After graduating from Kansas State University with a degree in home economics and journalism, she worked as a utility-company home economist touting how women could do it all with help from Redi-Kilowatt. But in real life she cooked hamburgers (on the good nights) and left messages for her husband, Jim, in the coffee-table dust.

Deciding there had to be a better way, she tried both full-time homemaking and part-time work—and discovered it truly is possible to live a good life on fewer than two paychecks.